THE FLORA OF THE CANARIES

TEXT BY
BRUNO FOGGI

PHOTOGRAPHY BY
ANDREA INNOCENTI

BONECHI

SUMMARY

Distribución:

COMERCIAL ATHENEUM S.A.
Joventud, 19 - 08830 Sant Boi de Llobregat (Barcelona) - España

Project and editorial conception: Casa Editrice Bonechi
Publication Manager: Monica Bonechi
Picture research: Alberto Andreini
Graphic design: Maria Rosanna Malagrinò
Make-up: Alberto Douglas Scotti
Editing: Patrizia Fabbri

Text: Bruno Foggi
Translation: Christina Coster-Longman

Map: Studio Grafico Daniela Mariani - Pistoia

Photographs from the archives of Casa Editrice Bonechi
taken by Andrea Innocenti.

© Copyright by Casa Editrice Bonechi, Via Cairoli 18/B Florence – Italy
Tel. +39 055 576841 – Fax +39 055 5000766
e-mail: bonechi@bonechi.it
Internet: www.bonechi.it

Printed in Italy by Centro Stampa Editoriale Bonechi.

ISBN 88-8029-638-8

* * *

INTRODUCTION

The archipelago of the Canary Islands lies in the Atlantic Ocean, 100 kilometres west of the Moroccan coast. It consists of seven large islands (Tenerife, Fuerteventura, Gran Canaria, Lanzarote, La Palma, La Gomera and Hierro) and four smaller ones (La Graciosa, Alegranza, Lobos and Montaña Clara), plus a chain of small rocks.

The archipelago was formed through the process of continental drift during the mid Cretaceous period (about 100 million years ago), when the African plate rotated with respect to the European one, provoking the uplift of the Alps. Rocks dating back to this period, and thus the most ancient part of the

archipelago, have been found at Fuerteventura. Subsequent stages of the islands' formation were the result of huge volcanic eruptions which occurred between the Miocene (19 million years ago) and the Pleistocene (0.5 million years ago). The oldest islands are those nearest the African Coast, whilst leaving the coast and proceeding seaward the island are of increasingly recent formation. From East to West, the sea surrounding the islands also becomes deeper; the depth of the sea is about 1,000 metres between the African coast and Lanzarote but 4,000 metres off La Palma. Consequently, proceeding from East to West, the archipelago gains more and more in oceanic characteristics whilst losing its continental ones.

Because of this peculiar geographical position, types of tropical and subtropical vegetation have managed to survive which once also occurred within the Mediterranean Basin but which disappeared after two major catastrophes. The first was the desertification in the late Miocene (Messiniano 8-9 million years ago) as a result of the orogenesis of the mountain chain corresponding to the Atlas Mountains and the Sierra Nevada of today, a phenomenon which brought a lower water supply from the Atlantic and consequently a drier and cooler climate to the surrounding lands. This was followed by a series of glacial cycles during the interval between the Pliocene and Pleistocene (1.5-0.1 million years ago) which cooled the land over the entire northern hemisphere with the consequent disappearance from Southern Europe and the Mediterranean lands of those subtropical types which had managed to survive the events of the Miocene. Other islands in the Atlantic Ocean also experienced these geological phenomena: the Azores, Madeira, the Salvajes Islands and Capoverde, which, together with the Canaries, form the biogeographical region known as Macaronesia.

The cycle of volcanic eruptions and subsequent erosion of the volcanic cones by the elements have given a particular character to the relief of the archipelago. The islands rise abruptly from the sea with their shear slopes, grooved by the many streams which flow in deep chasms called "barrancos". The result of the prolonged action of water, these chasms run down the main volcanic structure in an almost radial pattern. At their estuaries, the coasts are low and only rarely formed of sand deposits; for the most part they consist of platforms of rocky, volcanic material. The mountains are often very high, reaching their maximum in Tenerife with the peak of Teide rising to 3,718 metres, making it the highest volcano in Europe.

When the first people to visit the "Lucky Archipelago" saw the fire and smoke exuding from Teide, they called Tenerife "The Island of Hell". Fortunately this name did not pass into history, nor is there any record of it on the geographical maps. Its present name seems to be linked to a poem by Viana, who described the mountain as "tener-ife" - the mountain with snow. Snow and fire are in fact the two extremes which characterise the entire archipelago and testify the almost double nature of the Canaries. Indeed, the marked altitudinal range of the volcanoes are responsible for the great climatic contrasts typical of these islands.

The wet, cool air currents from the West and North-west, the Trade Winds, bring a cool wet, typically oceanic climate to the windward slopes of the islands, favouring a hardy and luxuriant vegetation. Altitudes between 300 and 1,500 metres feel the effect of the Trade Winds the most; below this level their effect is only slight, whilst over this altitude they are almost negligible and the climate is dry with very hot summers and harsh winters.

The slopes facing Africa are not only excluded from the benefits of the Trade Winds, which die out on the western slopes, they also feel the influence of the hot and dry winds blowing from the Sahara and are thus extremely dry. These marked climatic contrasts have favoured the islands' rich biodiversity.

Man's agricultural exploitation of the Canaries has undoubtedly been influenced by this situation. No certain data are available about who were the first people to colonise the islands, but in all probability the first settlers had North African somatic characters and they are known as the Guanches or Canarios. They had a Neolithic type of culture, so lived by simple sustainable agriculture and certainly in harmony with nature. Phoenicians, Persians and Carthaginians probably landed on the island in about 500 BC, but Pliny the Elder was the first to tell about an expedition to the "Lucky Islands" by Juba, Prince of Mauretania in the times of the Emperor Augustus. During the late Middle Ages, ships from Genoa and Majorca reached the islands, with Fernandez de Lugo as captain under the service of the Catholic Kings, who at the end of 1496 finally conquered the islands and incorporated them in the Crown of Castilla. The lands were divided and thus the transformation of the vegetation and landscape of the archipelago first began. The islands underwent massive deforestation to make room for growing cereals, in particular, sugar cane, vineyards, and orchards which flourished on the wet slopes where conditions were ideal for their cultivation. On the higher slopes, agriculture gave way to grazing, which exerted strong pressure on the autoctonous floral heritage.

With the increase in transatlantic traffic, the Canaries became a compulsory port of call for ships on their way to Spain from Latin America. Many species of exotic plants, both alimentary and ornamental, broke their journey on the archipelago, which thus became a sort of acclimatising garden. As a result, many species from Central and Southern America became part of the local flora, sometimes even taking its place. At present there are as many as 500 species of naturalised exotic flora in the Canaries, many of which live in areas of human settlement.

Over the last few years, traditional methods of agriculture have been abandoned and man-built spaces have increased. With the expansion of towns and industry and growing demographic pressures, linked especially with the tourist industry, the environment has deteriorated badly. The expansion of man-centred interests over the natural heritage, like the construction of roads, has seriously cut down the amount of the ecosystems originally present in the archipelago to just

20% of the total surface area. A symbolic example is Argyranthemum coronopifolium, an endemism found only in the tiny area of Teno Point (Tenerife): the construction of an asphalt road has separated individuals of the same population so they can no longer cross pollinate. Under the new conditions, the number of seeds and thus new individuals is falling more and more and consequently the species is tending to disappear. The different types of volcanic material forming the soil and the great variety in climates, plus the action of man have produced a highly varied and typical vegetation and landscape capable of maintaining a marked diversity of species.

The first important contribution to the knowledge of the natural heritage of these islands was the treatise by Webb & Berthelot. P.B. Webb (1793-1854) was a rich English landowner whose love of botany led him to travel the world. On his journey from Madeira to Brazil, in 1828 he stopped at Tenerife where he met S. Berthelot (1794-1880), who had already been collecting insects and plants of the islands for some years. Berthelot so ignited a love of the nature of the Canary Islands that Webb stayed at Tenerife for two years, forsaking his journey to Brazil. The following twenty years, together with Berthelot, were dedicated to writing his monumental work Histoire Naturelle des Iles Canaries (Natural History of the Canary Islands) which was published in Paris in 106 instalments between 1835 and 1850. The work, containing 287 lithographs, is in three volumes dedicated to the ethnography, geography, zoology and botany of the Canary and other islands of Macaronesia. The work lists 1,116 species of plants found in the archipelago, 232 of which described for the first time. The enormous amount of material collected over this expedition, to which should be added the huge number of specimens which Webb bought from several researchers, is now kept in the Webb Herbarium of Florence University, Italy as Webb wished, after his death. The Herbarium of Florence is therefore of primary historical and biological importance to those interested in the study of the flora of these islands.

At present, the flora of the Canary Islands consists of approximately 2,000 species, 520 of which can be considered endemic and as many as 593 rare or under threat of extinction. Many of these species belong to genera and subgenera not found outside of the Canaries or the other Macaronesian Islands. These groups have undergone speciation, induced by the different types of habitat, e.g. Aeonium (38 species), Echium (28), Argyranthemum (22) and Sonchus subgenus Dendrosonchus (19). This great diversity can be an important genetic resource in the future for new plants for agricultural, horticultural and medicinal purposes if they are protected from, the often inconsiderate, human intervention.

The scope of this short guide is to introduce the reader to some of the most characteristic species of this great biodiversity. To do this, we have divided the species according to their natural environment; descriptions of each plant are preceded by a brief introduction to its typical habitat. The descriptions are illustrated with a wide range of photographs. As the final aim is to know this highly valuable, from the scientific and naturalistic point of view, heritage, we have provided some information on the habitats and species which the European Community considers particularly important and worthy of protection (European Community Directive 43/92).

THE FLORA OF THE CANARIES

Several habitats or ecosystems can be recognised in the Canary Islands, each with its own typical species. The most important of these are illustrated and given a specific description. The following habitats are described:
Coastal; dry; laurel-leaf woodland; pinewoods; the highlands; cliffs and rocks; cultivated areas and wasteland; towns and gardens.

The main characteristics of all these ecosystems have been described, enabling the reader to easily recognise the habitat in which he or she finds him/herself. Description of the most interesting or common plants follows together with an illustration in the same order as which they are mentioned in the text. In the section on towns and gardens, on the contrary, plant names are given in alphabetical order.

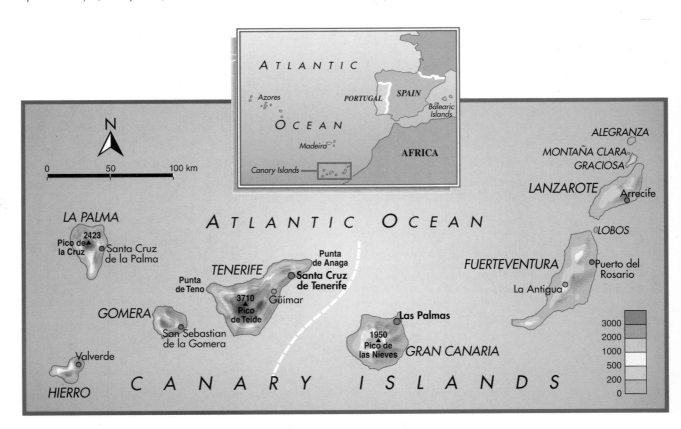

COASTAL HABITATS

The species growing in this habitat are highly characteristic and are not affected by the sea water, either directly or as sea spray carried by the winds. There are two types of coasts: low and either sandy or with salt lagoons, or high and rocky.

The first type gives coastal ecosystems with shrubs 30 to 100 cm high, with typically succulent branches and practically no or barely formed leaves, transformed into thick, fleshy scales. The branches and leaves are succulent because they must store large amounts of water to dilute the salt content in soil solutions. The species typical of this habitat occurring in the Canaries for the most part are the same as those found throughout the Mediterranean. Among these, *Zygophyllum fontanesii* deserves particular mention because of its Saharan-Canary distribution. Its occurrence in the archipelago gradually falls from East to West.

The second type of coast presents an ecosystem in direct contact with sea spray and the coenoses are dominated by *Astydamia latifolia*. Here species belonging to the genus *Limonium* can be found, among which

Right: Zygophyllum fontanesii *association; below: a view of the beautiful Tenerife coast near Guimar.*

Limonium fruticans and *L. ar-borescens* are particularly interesting. In the highest coastal areas, the plant communities are characterised by *Argyranthemum frutescens* subsp. *succulentum*, *Frankenia ericifolia* and *F. laevis* subsp. *capitata*. This type of community tends to gradually disappear further from the areas under the effect of the sea spray, but it sometimes mingles with the Euphorbia stands with *Euphorbia canariensis* or *E. balsamifera*, which can descend with the rocks as far as sea level.

The sand often forms little heaps between the rocks, thus creating microhabitats characterised by species which can tolerate both arid and salty condtitions; these plants are called psamhalophytes. Among these is *Lotus glaucus*, a small herbaceous plant with showy yellow flowers.

Many plants of these coastal habitats are endemic to the Canary Islands. For this reason the European Community (Directive 43/92) considers these habitats to be important and worth protecting.

Above: the cliffs of Teno and below a view of Teno Point (Tenerife).

1

ZYGOPHYLLUM FONTANESII WEBB & BERTH. ☐1

(Zygophyllaceae) Babosa

Shrub up to one metre in height
with opposite branches and
leaves. Leaves succulent, fleshy
and trefoil.
Flowers small and solitary.
A halophyte, i.e. able to live using
water at the same or even higher
saline concentration as sea water.

ASTYDAMIA LATIFOLIA (L. FIL.) BAILL. ☐2

(Umbelliferae) Acelga del Mar

This herbaceous plant with small,
yellowish flowers lives on the
rocky coastlines of all the islands.
It is easily recognised by its rather
large, succulent, pinnate leaves
which may be toothed to various
degrees. The flowers are arranged
in umbrella-shaped inflorescences
with about 15 rays.

2

LIMONIUM ARBORESCENS (BROUSS.) O.KUNTZE [3]
(Plumbaginaceae)
Perpetuas marinas

Small shrub characterised by a very strong, lower woody portion and long, herbaceous stems carrying the flowers in branched inflorescences at the tip. The plant grows to 2,5 metres in height, the leaves are large, ovate and hairless, with a long petiole and fleshy blade. Flowering stems are much branched but compact with lateral growths running their entire length. Flowers pink. This very rare species is endemic to the Island of Tenerife and is declining in number because of human pressure along the coasts.

LIMONIUM FRUTICANS (WEBB) O.KUNTZE [4]
(Plumbaginaceae)
Perpetuas marinas

Considered by some authors as only a local variety of the former species, from which it differs for its generally smaller size. Also a rare species and in danger of extinction. Endemic to Tenerife where it can be found at El Fraele and Los Silos.

3

4

5

ARGYRANTHEMUM FRUTESCENS (L.) SCH. BIP. SUBSP. SUCCULENTUM HUMPHR. [5]
(Compositae) Margaritas

Shrub with characteristic fleshy and succulent leaves like the other species which live in the same type of habitat. This "Succulent Daisy" reaches 80 centimetres in height, its branches are thin and at the tip carry the clusters typical of the Compositae family. These clusters consist of central yellow flowers and lateral ones carrying white ligules. Endemic to the Island of Tenerife.

FRANKENIA LAEVIS L. SUBSP. *CAPITATA* WEBB & BERTH. 6 8
(Frankeniaceae) Sapera

Small creeping shrub, this Sea-Heath has typically small, fleshy leaves, often reddish like the branches. Leaves opposite and pubescent due to tiny, short hairs. The flowers are arranged at the tip of the short branches and vary from pale pink to whitish in colour.

6

FRANKENIA ERICIFOLIA CHR., SM. & DC. 7
(Frankeniaceae) Albohol

Very similar to previous species with which it often occurs, but from which it differs on account of the smaller, usually white flowers arranged along the entire length of the branches. General appearance of a more or less compact plant.

7↑ 9↓

LOTUS GLAUCUS AIT. 9
(Leguminosae) Corazoncillo

Small herbaceous perennial, with composite leaves formed by 5 leaflets, at a maximum 5 millimetres long. Pale yellow flowers arranged on long stalks at the leaf axil, either singly or in pairs. Endemic to Macaronesia.

8

DRY HABITATS

This ecosystem has developed almost uniformly between the coast and the first mountain slopes of the islands up to 700 metres. It is characterised by a hot, dry sub-desert climate with an annual rain fall of 150-250 millimetres and annual mean temperatures almost constantly over 20°C. The vegetation can be compared to that of the dry areas of Sudan, Ethiopia, Arabia and Iran and is typical of the steppes of Africa.

These areas are characterised by open associations of succulent shrubs, which are divided into various types of communities, each dominated by particular species belonging to the genus *Euphorbia*, the most common of which is *E. canariensis* with its classical "cactus" appearance. It is a succulent, whose leaves have been transformed into small spines arranged along the keels of the trunk, which can be quadrangular or pentagonal in section. Because the plant has no leaves, photosynthesis is performed by the trunk itself and the branches, which are therefore green. These organs are also responsible for storing water, which is slowly released during dry periods. A liana, *Periploca laevigata*, often lives on the branches of *Euphorbia canariensis*. Besides this species, this belt of vegetation is also characterised by *Campylanthus salsoloides*, *Euphorbia obtusifolia*, *Ploca-*

Left: two views of Teno with, top, **Euphorbia canariensis.** *Large picture:* **E. canariensis** *in Guimar Valley, Island of Tenerife.*

ma pendula, Argyranthemum gracile, Allagopappus dichotomus, Sonchus canariensis and *Kleinia neriifolia.* The last species is very similar to species of the genus *Euphorbia* but can be distinguished from the latter, in the absence of flowers, by the lack of the typical whitish latex.

Several species belonging to the genus *Euphorbia,* but which do not look like cacti, can be found within this hot and dry, wide belt of vegetation. These are woody plants between 1 and 3 metres high, characterised by a well evident, small, more or less prostrate trunk from which a series of branches all depart at the same height and which in turn tend to branch out dichotomously. The end result resembles a miniature tree with short trunk and an almost spherical crown, looking like a candelabra or an umbrella turned inside out. Together with others, this species forms various types of plant associations, depending on the local characteristics of the environment.

In the hottest and driest areas *E. balsamifera* coenoses occur. This beautiful plant forms open associations with other interesting plants, among which two graminaceous grasses: *Tricholaena teneriffae,* distributed in Africa and the Canaries, and *Hyparrhenia hirta,* with a widespread distribution covering all the tropical and subtropical areas of Africa and Asia. *Euphorbia aphylla, Ceropegia dichotoma* and *Argyranthemum coronopifolium,* on the contrary, are typical of associations developing on the rocky coasts which still feel the influence of the sea. These areas are called aerohaline, since they are connected with the sea-spray transported by marine winds. In the Masca Valley, on the north-west slopes of the Island

**Right: Dry habitat in the area of Malpais de Guimar.
Below: Euphorbia balsamifera *coenosis near the coast
of Guimar, Island of Tenerife.***

of Tenerife, at between 700 and 1,100 metres altitude, communities dominated by *Euphorbia atropurpurea* develop, where *Retama raetam*, *Echium aculeatum* and *Lavandula canariensis* grow in association. This candelabra-like Euphorbia is endemic to Tenerife and is easily distinguished from the others by its purple coloured flowers.

Natural palms can also be found in this belt of vegetation, now very rare in all the islands of the archipelago on account of human intervention which has markedly reduced the sort of habitats suitable for the Canaries Palm, *Phoenix canariensis*. This species lives preferably on deep alluvial soils where the water table remains near the surface for much of the year. The rare stations of the Canaries Palm must therefore be sought in the beds of the "barrancos", where

even during the dry season, a certain amount of water still remains in the soil. The only natural populations of the Canaries Palm can be found in the following localities: Haria, Lanzarote; Rio Palmas, Fuerteventura; Fataga and Maspalomas, Gran Canaria; Gran Rey Valley, Canadas de Hurona, La Gomera; Masca, Tenerife; Brena Alata, La Palma.

Top: **Euphorbia balsamifera;** *in the* **smaller photograph: panorama of** **Guimar Valley.**

In some of the areas where *Phoenix canariensis* grows can also be found wild *Dracaena draco*, the so-called "Canaries Dragon", another species which has become very rare because of the presence of man in these areas with a hot wet microclimate.

The natural *P. canariensis* palm stands are a habitat of primary importance within the European Community (Directive 43/92).

In areas where organic substances have accumulated, communities of nitrogen loving shrubs dominated by *Launaea arborescens* occur, a species easily seen even along the sides of main roads. This type of vegetation has a very widespread distribution, from Iran to the Canaries, passing through the hottest parts of the Mediterranean basin. *Gonospermum fruticosum*, *Lavandula buchii* and *Lavatera acerifolia* also occur in the same areas.

Another coenosis of this type develops on the slopes of the Anaga massif, in the north-eastern part of Tenerife, dominated by *Argyranthemum broussonetii*, *Artemisia thuscula*, *Lobularia canariensis*, *Plantago arborescens* and *Echium simplex*.

Right: Euphorbia atropurpurea *in Masca Valley.* **Below,** Euphorbia aphylla *on the majestic cliffs at Teno.*

EUPHORBIA CANARIENSIS L. [10][12]
(Euphorbiaceae)
Cardon

The most characteristic plant of the hot dry habitat in the lower areas of the Canary Islands. A small tree, up to 3-4 metres tall, with succulent, green cactus-like trunk, square or pentagonal in section.
The leaves are transformed into thorns, up to 5-14 millimetres long and arranged in tufts of three or four. The flowers are a green to red colour. An endemic species to the Canaries but rare in the eastern islands.

PERIPLOCA LAEVIGATA AIT. [11]
(Asclepiadaceae)
Cornical

This plant is woody at the base with long herbaceous shoots which climb round the trunks of other plants, especially *E. canariensis*. Oval-lanceolate, opposite leaves with pointed tip. Bicoloured flowers with the inner portion brown-purple and external portion greenish in colour.

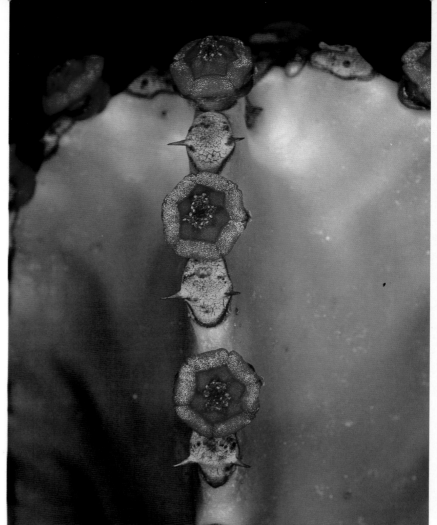

10↑ 11↓

KLEINIA NERIIFOLIA HAW. [16]
(Compositae) Berode

Shrub with succulent trunk up to one metre tall. The branches are jointed, i.e. they bear a series of constrictions which makes them look like a string of sausages. The leaves are arranged in a tuft at the tip of the branches; deciduous, thickish, more or less lanceolate and up to 12 centimetres long. The flowers are arranged in whitish inflorescences but it is very difficult to see this plant in flower. An endemic plant to the archipelago.

13

14↑ 15↓

CAMPYLANTHUS SALSOLOIDES (L. FIL.) ROTH [13]
(Scrophulariaceae) Romero marino

Shrub up to 2 metres tall. Leaves linear and succulent. Flowers varying in colour from pink to pale blue to whitish and arranged in loose inflorescences, sometimes curved. An endemic plant to the Canaries.

EUPHORBIA OBTUSIFOLIA POIR. [14] [15]
(Euphorbiaceae) Tabaiba amarga

Like the other species of the genus *Euphorbia* which can be found in the driest parts of the Canaries, *E. obtusifolia* is a small tree characterised by the short, always well evident trunk and by a wide, almost round crown with branches that carry the leaves in tufts at the tip. A common plant, especially in the hottest and driest areas, up to 2 meters high with upright trunk. Leaves linear, with sharp tip, up to 7 centimetres long and no more than 6 millimetres wide. Flowers arranged in inflorescences called cyathiums, with pale green bracts. This species is distributed in North Africa and the Canaries.

17

18↑ 19↓

PLOCAMA PENDULA
AIT. 17 18
(Rubiaceae) Balo

Small tree up to 5 meters tall, characterised by a small, but well evident trunk and loose, open crown with arched, flexible and drooping branches. Long-lasting, filiform leaves up to 5-6 centimetres long and pale green in colour. Whitish, solitary flowers only occurring at the ends of the branches. An endemic species to the Canaries, tends to occur less proceeding from the western to the eastern islands. Extremely dangerous milk, or latex, especially for the eyes.

ARGYRANTHEMUM GRACILE
SCH.BIP. 19
(Compositae) Margaritas

This *Argyranthemum* looks very much like the others except for its smaller size, filiform leaves and smaller inflorescences. Endemic to Tenerife where it is fairly common below 700 metres altitude.

ALLAGOPAPPUS DICHOTOMUS
(L. FIL.) CASS. 20
(Compositae) Madama

Bush up to one meter high with yellowish stems. Leaves lanceolate, mucronate tip, with notched edges; sticky due to essential oils. Flowers arranged in yellow composite inflorescences which are in turn arranged in clusters at the tip of the branches. Endemic to the Canary Islands but does not occur at Hierro, Lanzarote or Fuerteventura.

20

21

SONCHUS CANARIENSIS (SCH.BIP.) BOULOS 21 22
(Compositae) Cerraja arborea

Belongs to the arboreal *Sonchus* group (*Dendrosonchus* section), of which it is the largest. Shrub consisting of an erect stem, straight or with two or three ramifications, each bearing a rosette of leaves at the tip, similar to that carried by the herbaceous *Sonchus* at ground level. The stem, in this case, reaches 3 meters in height. Leaves pinnate, toothed, up to 15-20 centimetres long. The inflorescences are carried on one or two branches which leave the centre of the rosette, each of which can bear up to 100-150 little yellow-coloured composite inflorescences. Endemic to the Canaries.

22

EUPHORBIA BALSAMIFERA AIT. 23 24
(Euphorbiaceae) Tabaiba dulce

Although it can reach up to 2 meters in height, this species always has a very branched creeping trunk, sometimes very robust. Leaves always carried in tufts at the tips of the branches, reaching a maximum length of 2.5 centimetres. Inflorescences have yellowish green bracts. As well as the Canaries, also occurs in North Africa and Somalia. This *Euphorbia* also produces latex like the other members of this genus, which has been used for setting milk.

23

24

25

26

TRICHOLAENA TENERIFFAE (L. FIL.) LINK [25]
(Graminaceae)
Cerillo blanco

Perennial graminaceous grass up to 60 centimetres tall, characteristic for its whitish and pubescent spikes. Its distribution covers North Africa and the Canaries, where it is fairly common in the hotter and more arid areas.

HYPARRHENIA HIRTA (L.) STAPF [26]
(Graminaceae)

Species of the genus *Hyparrhenia* are found in the tropical countries of all the continents, where they form part of the flora of the great savannahs. Some of the species of the genus can reach 6 metres in height, e.g. *H. cymbaria* (L.) Stapf. *H. hirta* is among the smaller species, reaching just 60 centimetres. It can be recognised by the ears which are arranged at the tip of the culm, like the fingers of an open hand, and supported by a red-violet coloured leaf. It occurs especially in the hottest, driest and most degraded areas. *H. arrhenobasis* (Hochst. ex Steud.) Stapf, also occurs in the Canary Islands and is often found in association with *H. hirta*, but it is not certain whether they are two distinct species or not.

EUPHORBIA APHYLLA BROUSS. EX WILLD. [27]
(Euphorbiaceae) Tabaiba salvaje

Small shrub no more than 50 centimetres high. The stem carries very small, greyish green jointed branches in opposite, dichotomous ramifications, or in whorls. Leaves sparse, small and precociously caducous, so it is as if the plant lacks any. Endemic to the Canary Islands.

27

28

29

CEROPEGIA DICHOTOMA HAW. 28
(Asclepiadaceae)
Cardoncillo

Small shrub with succulent stems no higher than 60 centimetres, practically with no leaves for most of the year. The stem is pale greenish-grey-brown, smooth with several constrictions which make it look like a long string of sausages. The flowers are gathered in groups of two to seven at the tip of one of the previous year's stems. Species endemic to Tenerife.

ARGYRANTHEMUM CORONOPIFOLIUM (WILLD.) HUMPHR. 29
(Compositae) Margaritas

Creeping shrub no higher than 40-50 centimetres. Succulent, hairless, oblanceolate leaves, toothed at the tip. Flowers grouped in composite inflorescences, 2.5 centimetres in diameter, with the central portion yellow and with white-cream ligulate flowers.
One to eight inflorescences. Extremely rare plant found only near Teno, in a limited area between the rocks of Fraele and Bellavista Point, Island of Tenerife on the wet basalt cliffs between 50 and 200 metres altitude. Should be considered a threatened species and therefore deserves protection.

EUPHORBIA ATROPURPUREA (BROUSS.) WEBB & BERTH. 30
(Euphorbiaceae)
Tabaiba mejorera

This plant can reach two metres in height. The leaves are oblanceolate, glaucous green, grouped in tufts at the branch tips. The flowers are arranged in wide inflorescences with deep purple bracts, rarely yellowish. Fruits are dark red or brown. This beautiful *Euphorbia* occurs only in the south-west part of Tenerife, at between 300 and 1,200 metres altitude.

30

LAVANDULA CANARIENSIS MILL. [33]
(Labiatae) Hierba del risco

Endemic species to the Canary Islands, this shrub is woody at the base with erect herbaceous branches, ending in inflorescences. Opposite, pubescent and pinnate leaves, green-greyish in colour with rounded lateral appendices. Violet flowers gathered in long, spiked and branched inflorescences.

31

32

RETAMA RAETAM (FORSSK.) WEBB & BERTH. [31]
(Leguminosae) Retama blanca

Species distributed in North Africa and the Canary Islands excluding Lanzarote and Fuerteventura. A shrub up to 5 metres high, with flexible, reed-like, green-greyish branches and loose crown. The young branches are jointed and shiny. Almost always without leaves, which only appear after a rainy season. White flowers with strong smell of sweet honey, arranged in large, showy inflorescences. Highly valued decorative plant and the flowers are sold in the local markets.

ECHIUM ACULEATUM POIR. [32]
(Boraginaceae) Taginaste

Small tree up to 3 metres high, with a short trunk and roundish branched crown. The leaves are linear and tend to be carried high near the flowers. Pale blue to white flowers gathered in short, spiked inflorescences. Endemic to the Canaries, but absent from Lanzarote and Fuerteventura.

33

PHOENIX CANARIENSIS
HORT. EX CHAB. [34] [35] [36]
(Palmae) Palma

A palm up to 12 metres high, rarely 15, characterised by a tuft of leaves carried at the top of a straight trunk. It is almost always regularly pruned so the heads usually have only a few leaves, whilst non-pruned specimens are shorter but have more leaves, up to 60-100. The leaves are pinnate and very long, up to 7 metres, with 100 to 150 pairs of coriaceous, but flexible, leaflets, which are provided with a double series of extremely hard, yellowish short thorns at the base. Small flowers gathered in dense inflorescences which are branched and up to a metre and a half long; male flowers are whitish, female flowers yellowish. The fruits are similar to dates, "tamanares", oval and 1.5-2 centimetres long but with not much flesh. They are edible but of little value and are therefore not picked. When they fall they are eaten by birds, mice and pigs. Very young leaves can be eaten raw in salads. At La Gomera, "palm honey" is used which is produced by preventing the flowers to form. Successfully adopted as an ornamental species for parks and gardens. On those islands where the date palm (*P. dactylifera* L.) is grown, hybrids of the two palms can be found. Together with the Dragon, this plant can be considered the symbol of the Canary Islands, even though it is found less and less in the wild.

34

37

DRACAENA DRACO (L.) L. 37
(Dracaenaceae) Drago

A tree-like plant with massive, short thick trunk which divides into a series of almost dichotomous branches, each carrying a tuft of leaves in a rosette at the tip. The leaves are linear, rigid, green-grey in colour and up to 60 centimetres long in large specimens. Small, whitish flowers gathered in a drooping inflorescence. Round, fleshy, orange coloured fruits. The plant is an endemic of the Macaronesian Islands. There are many legends attached to the "Canaries Dragon": mediaeval manuscripts

narrate that the blood-red lymph, or "sangre de dragón", which escapes when the bark is cut, is magical and endowed with medical properties capable or curing ulcers and dysentery. There has been a lot of speculation as to how long a Dracena can live: Alexander von Humboldt, one of the earliest explorers of the Canary Islands, tells that a plant in the Orotava Valley which was destroyed by a hurricane in 1867, was more than 6,000 years old. Fenzl, in an article in the "Gardener's Chronicle", writes that the circumference of the same plant reached 78 feet (27 metres). Along with the Canary Palm, it only grows

wild in some particular areas where a few individuals occur which differ somewhat from those commonly seen at Icod de los Vinos. *D. draco* can be considered a living fossil and is therefore a protected species in the habitat where it occurs spontaneously.

38

39

LAUNAEA ARBORESCENS (BATT.) MURB. 38
(Compositae) Ahulaga

Bush, up to 70 centimetres high, whose short branches have been transformed into small thorns. Leaves scanty, small and glaucous, slightly lobed. Flowers gathered in small, yellow coloured inflorescences (1 centimetre in diameter).

GONOSPERMUM FRUTICOSUM (BUCH) LESS. 39
(Compositae) Corona de la Reina

Another composite which can easily be distinguished from *Launea* on account of its larger inflorescences (up to 5 centimetres in diameter), by the transparent scales of the sheath and its leaves which appear grey due to the thick covering of tomentum. The *Gonospermum* shrub can reach up to a metre and a half in height, has pinnate leaves and yellow coloured inflorescences.
G. fruticosum is endemic to the Canary Islands.

LAVANDULA BUCHII WEBB 40
(Labiatae) Mato risco

Easily recognised both by is pale blue to violet flowers and for its pinnate leaves covered by a thick and dense layer of hairs, giving it a greyish hue and a cotton like touch. It differs from the other species of the genus *Lavandula* found on the Canaries on account of its hairy leaves and its calyx which is longer than the underlying bracts.

LAVATERA ACERIFOLIA CAV. 41
(Malvaceae) Malva silvestre

Species endemic to the Canary Islands, distinguished from the rarer *L. phoenicea* Vent. by its flowers which are darker and narrower at the base. A shrub up to 2.5 metres high with large, palmate leaves with irregularly toothed lobes and very long petiole. Flowers large (up to 7-8 centimetres in diameter), mauve, darker at the base, rarely whitish in colour.

42

43

44

ARGYRANTHEMUM BROUSSONETII (PERS.) HUMPHR. 42

(Compositae) Margaritas

Shrub up to 1.2 metres tall, very robust and compact. Leaves up to 16 centimetres long, elliptical-obovate, bi-pinnate, hairless or with just a few hairs along the midrib. Flowers arranged in inflorescences, the central part of which is yellow whilst the ligulate flowers are white. The species *A. broussonetii* is endemic to Tenerife.

ARTEMISIA THUSCULA CAV. 43

(Compositae) Ajenjo

Small shrub easily recognised by the strong smell of incense the leaves give when they are rubbed. Reaching up to a metre in height, the leaves are a silver grey colour and usually flaccid. Flowers in small, golden-yellow, very compact inflorescences.
A. thuscula is endemic to the Canary Islands.

45

46

ECHIUM SIMPLEX DC. 47
(Boraginaceae) Arrebol

An enormous, perennial and sometimes biennial herbaceous plant with a short, non-branched stem. The linear, lanceolate leaves are very hispid due to the short silvery hairs and are arranged in a thick basal rosette. The flower scape is leafy and up to 2 metres high. The white flowers are arranged in a long, spiked inflorescence. Endemic to Tenerife.

LOBULARIA CANARIENSIS (WEBB) BORGEN 44 45
(Cruciferae) Hierba de la rabia

Small, woody shrub endemic to Macaronesia. The petals vary from white to pink, and the sepals from green to reddish. *Lobularia canariensis* is a highly variable species and several subspecies have been recognised: *L. canariensis* subsp. *canariensis*, *L. canariensis* subsp. *intermedia* (Webb) Borgen, *L. canariensis* subsp. *palmensis* (Christ) Bergen and *L. canariensis* subsp. *microsperma* Bergen. It is difficult to distinguish between these subspecies and the only characters which can be used are the variations in the colour of the sepals.

PLANTAGO ARBORESCENS POIR. 46
(Plantaginaceae) Pinillo

Small, creeping shrub reaching at the most 60 centimetres in height, woody and very branched at the base. The woody branches give out herbaceous shoots with very thick spiked inflorescences, consisting of extremely small flowers with scarious sepals and petals, which when mature turn a yellow colour due to the anthers. *P. arborescens* is endemic to the Canary Islands.

47

LAUREL-LEAF WOODLAND

The flora of the wet and mountainous areas of the Canary Islands consists of luxuriant woods of evergreen, laurel-leaf trees; in Spanish they are typically called "monte verde" (green mountains) or "laurisilva canariense". The North-westerly Trade Winds bring a constant supply of wet air which, as it rises up the mountain ranges, condenses to form a blanket of cloud, which varies in thickness depending on the season. This practically permanent girdle of mist creates the optimum microclimate for forests dominated by evergreen, woody species of subtropical origin to develop on the exposed slopes to the North and North-west. The area for the potential development of "green mountain" vegetation falls within the belt between 500 and 1,600 metres altitude on the north-west slopes of the more western islands, although under particularly favourable conditions such as occur on the Anaga massif at Tenerife, the lower limit can fall to 100 metres above sea level. The Laurel-leaf woodland of the Canary Islands can be considered as a Paleo-flora relict of the wet sub-tropical vegetation which covered most of Southern Europe and Northern Africa up to the end the Tertiary (late Miocene and beginning of the Pliocene). Indeed, fossils of plants belonging to the genera occurring today in the Canaries have been found in many of the countries bordering the Mediterranean basin, e.g. Spain, France and Italy.

Top: laurel-leaf woodlands on the Anaga massif.
Left and bottom: the woods at Las Mercedes, Island of Tenerife.

View of Santa Cruz of Tenerife, from the Pico del Inglés.

The total extension of the laurel woodlands today does not exceed 6.7% of the area of the Islands. The best preserved forests can be found at several localities at La Gomera; Tenerife (Anaga, Los Silos, Guimar, Agua Arcia, San Antonio-Icod); La Palma (Las Sauces); Hierro (Ensenada El Golfo); Gran Canaria (Los Tiles). Literature mentions patches of this type of woodland at Fuerteventura (Riscos de Jandia) and Lanzarote (Riscos de Famara) but no traces of this type of vegetation remain today.

The laurel-leaf woodlands on each island has its own mixture of characteristic plants, mostly trees and shrubs, among which species belonging to the genus *Pericallis,* and particular fauna such as ground beetles (Carabidae) and the *Columba junionae* and *C. bollei* butterflies, in danger of extinction, which are only found at La Gomera, La Palma and Tenerife. For this reason the Canary Islands Laurel Forests are a priority for the European Community (Directive 43/92).

This type of vegetation shows signs of degradation as it occurs in areas particularly suitable for agriculture, although some large basins of Tenerife, La Gomera and La Palma can still boast substantial stands of this type of woodland. Among the most interesting and common species of trees are: *Laurus azorica*, *Apollonias barbujana* and *Maytenus canariensis*; whilst *Viburnum tinus* subsp. *rigidum*, *Hedera helix* subsp. *canariensis* and *Luzula canariensis* can be found in the underbrush. Typical herbaceous communities occur on the border of these woodlands, with *Isoplexis canariensis, Ranunculus cortusifolius, Pericallis cruenta, P. echinata, Vinca major* and *Sideritis macrostachys.*

On the steeper slopes and in the narrower and deeper crevices, especially among the rocks, some interesting ferns can be found in the underbrush including *Adiantum reniforme, Asplenium hemionitis* and *Davallia canariensis.* Still within the laurel-leaf woodland belt, but where the environmental conditions are less favourable, partly due to man, the "brezales" prevail. These are stands of shrubs dominated by heathers: *Erica ar-*

borea and *E. scoparia* subsp. *platycodon* often associated with *Myrica faya* and *Hypericum glandulosum.* The stands dominated by *Erica platycodon* reach their maximum development on the crests of the Anaga massif, in North Tenerife and the higher points of Inchereda, at Gomera. It should be underlined that the European Community considers the Macaronesian Island heathlands as a habitat of priority importance (Directive 43/92).

In the sunnier areas and where conditions have been even more altered by human intervention, formations of low shrubs develop, belonging to the *Leguminosae* family. These include *Adenocarpus foliolosus, Cytisus scoparius* and sometimes *Ulex europaeus,* a species which probably has only recently been introduced by man.

A picturesque view of a gorge on the Teno massif, Tenerife.

LAURUS AZORICA (SEUB.) FRANCO 48
(Lauraceae) Laurel

Endemic to the Macaronesian Islands but not found on Lanzarote or Fuerteventura where it seems to have become extinct due to human activity. The "Canaries Laurel" tree grows to between 10 and 20 metres in height, sometimes reaching 35 metres. The trunk is straight, the bark grey and generally smooth but can be tomentose on younger branches. Can reach a metre and a half in diameter (one laurel at La Gomera reaches 1.6 metres in diameter). Evergreen, bright green, coriaceous leaves up to 10-15 centimetres long and 4-5 centimetres wide. Axillary, showy, creamy-yellow flowers with greenish veins. The fruit looks like a small, blackish olive. Once used for charcoal production.

48

49

APOLLONIAS BARBUJANA (CAV.) BORNM. 49
(Lauraceae) Barbusano

Tree reaching 25-30 metres in height with characteristic round crown and grey, rough bark. Ovate-lanceolate, shiny, dark green leaves, 6-9 centimetres long and up to 4 centimetres wide, almost always spotted with warts. Small, white highly perfumed flowers. The fruits, or berries, resemble olives and turn from a red to blackish colour as they ripen. The "Barbusano" is an endemic tree to the Canaries and Madeira. It is particularly interesting because its nearest relative is *A. arnottii*, which grows in South India.

50

MAYTENUS CANARIENSIS (LOES.) KUNK. & SUND. [50]
(Celastraceae) Perarillo

Small tree no higher than
7-8 metres, which in rocky, cliff-like
places takes on the form of a
prostrate shrub. Irregular trunk with
dark, very rough bark, short, knotted
and crooked branches, crown small
and sparse. Shiny green, long-lasting
leaves with short petiole, ovate
blade and toothed edges. Small,
white flowers in axillary clusters
high on the branches. The fleshy
fruits are divided into three valves.
Endemic species to the Canaries.

VIBURNUM TINUS L. SUBSP. *RIGIDUM* (VENT.) P.SILVA [51]
(Caprifoliaceae) Afollado

Typical shrub of the laurel wood
underbrush, its presence is a sign of
good conservation of the tree layer
since it does not like much light. Up
to 5-6 metres high, the young
branches are hairy. Large, opposite

51

52

leaves (up to 20 centimetres long and 12 centimetres wide), very hairy and sometimes bristly and reddish when still young. Small, white and perfumed flowers arranged in rich end inflorescences. Endemic to the Canaries and can be used as an ornamental tree for gardens and hedges as long as in the shade.

LUZULA CANARIENSIS POIR. 53
(Juncaceae)

A perennial rush with graminaceous-like leaves characterised by long, whitish and soft hairs, especially on the basal portion of the leaf and along the edges of the leaf blade. The plant is no higher than half a metre and carries a compact inflorescence of small whitish, transparent looking flowers at the top. Endemic to the Canaries, where it is found in, and sometimes on the margins, of the laurel-leaf woodland, especially where *Erica scoparia* subsp. *platycodon* is abundant.

HEDERA HELIX L. SUBSP. CANARIENSIS (WILLD.) COUT. 52
(Araliaceae) Hedra

A woody, climbing plant which takes the place of the common *Hedera helix* subsp. *helix* in the Canary Islands, from which it can be distinguished only by a few minor characters.

53

56

57

ISOPLEXIS CANARIENSIS
(L.) LOUD. 58
(Scrophulariaceae) Crista de Gallo

A perennial figwort with woody
base up to a metre high.
Lanceolate, coriaceous and slightly
pubescent leaves. Large flowers
(about 3 centimetres long), bright
red-orange arranged in dense
inflorescences. *I. canariensis* is
endemic to the Canary Islands and
is found on Tenerife, La Gomera
and La Palma. On Gran Canaria a
further two species occur,
I. isabelliana (Webb & Berth.) Masf.
and *I. chalcantha* Svent. & O'Shan.,
which can be distinguished on
account of the size of the flowers
which never exceed 2 centimetres
and for the denser pubescence.

RANUNCULUS
CORTUSIFOLIUS **WILLD.** 54 56
(Ranunculaceae) Morgallana

It is quite easy to find some
beautiful, colourful plants along the
dappled margins of the laurel-leaf
woodlands. One such is
R. cortusifolius, easily recognised
by its large, yellow flowers.
A thickly haired, herbaceous plant
up to 60 centimetres high. Whilst
the apical leaves are lanceolate,
the basal leaves are roundish to
orbicular and up to 30 centimetres
wide. The flowers can reach
5 centimetres in diameter.

PERICALLIS ECHINATA
(L. FIL.) B.NORD. 55 57
(Compositae)

A herbaceous perennial
reaching 30-50 centimetres in
height, with orbicular, roundish
leaves from hairless to slightly
pubescent, carried on a petiole
with leafy growths. The
inflorescences are a pinkish
colour and reach
2.5 centimetres across.
Distribution: Island of Tenerife.

58

PERICALLIS CRUENTA (L'HER.) BOLLE 59
(Compositae)

Very similar to the previous species, but easily distinguished by its leaves which are crimson-pink on the lower page, due to the thick covering of hairs. Like the former, this species of *Pericallis* is only found on Tenerife.

59

VINCA MAJOR L. 60
(Asclepiadaceae)

The "Greater Periwinkle" is a species introduced by man, but which has easily become

60

naturalised in such an extremely favourable climate. A creeping plant, with evergreen, opposite leaves. Flowers purple blue or violet, not very large and characterised by the funnel-shaped corolla-tube reaching 15 millimetres depth and the broad petalled portion up to 5 centimetres across, which gives it a rather ornamental appearance. There are many cultivars.

SIDERITIS MACROSTACHYS POIR. 61
(Labiatae) Chagora

The genus *Sideritis* is represented by many species on the Canary Islands, some of them known for their very isolated, small populations which are difficult to find. *S. macrostachys* is also a very rare species which occurs on the wet rocks of the belt of laurel-leaf woodland in the Anaga area of Tenerife. It is a small shrub no more than a metre high, with very large, ovate leaves. The lower leaf page is whitish and felt-like on account of the thick layer of tomentum but the upper is greenish-grey. The flowers are whitish with shades of brown, but the calyx which is covered with the same white layer of hairs as the leaves, makes them rather ostentatious. The flowers are arranged in a dense, spiked inflorescence, sometimes branched at the base.

ADIANTUM RENIFORME L. [62]
(Adiantaceae)

Like *Asplenium*, this is a genus of fern with a cosmopolitan distribution, among which *A. capillus-veneris* (Maidenhair) is certainly the most famous. *A. reniforme* is a small fern with kidney shaped leaves, no larger than 4-5 centimetres wide, carried on a petiole which can reach up to 20 centimetres in length. This little fern lives in shady, warm and wet areas and so finds its optimum habitat between the rocks within the laurel-leaf woodlands. Its distribution is limited to the Macaronesian Islands.

62

63

ASPLENIUM HEMIONITIS L. [63]
(Aspleniaceae)

This fern lives in western Mediterranean countries and Macaronesia, and indeed is associated with very wet and rather hot habitats. The leaves are generally long with the base widening out like two great ears, with the petiole inserted in the middle.

DAVALLIA CANARIENSIS (L.) J. E. SM. [64]
(Davalliaceae)

This characteristic fern can be found on the dry walls and rocks within the laurel-leaf woodland belt. Easily recognisable on account of its long creeping rhizome which is completely covered with reddish hairs. The leaves, up to 45 centimetres long and 30 centimetres wide, are green. Like the other two ferns, the "Canary Davallia" is found in the western Mediterranean as far as Macaronesia.

64

65   66

67

ERICA ARBOREA L. 65 66
(Ericaceae) Brejo

A widely distributed species covering South Europe, the countries round the Mediterranean Sea, the Mountains of Central and East Africa and Macaronesia. It is always associated with soils poor in calcium, like those of volcanic origin. A small tree reaching 7-8 metres in height, especially in well preserved woodlands. Needle-shaped, rather rigid, small leaves (no more than 6-8 millimetres long), dark green in colour. Minute, pinkish-white flowers, arranged in numerous groups at the tips of the highest branches, giving the plant a beautiful appearance when in flower so that it is often employed as an ornamental species. The "Heather Tree" is typical of high shrub stands called "fayal-brezal", where it is associated with other species. In extremely degraded conditions, especially after fire, it can become invasive and give rise to low shrubland, almost monospecific stands.

ERICA SCOPARIA L. SUBSP. *PLATYCODON* (WEBB & BERTH.) A.HANS & KUNK. 67
(Ericaceae) Tejo

Two species of heather are found on the Canary Islands: *E. arborea* (brejo) and *E. Scoparia* subsp. *platycodon* (tejo). Although the general appearance of the two plants, which often occur together, is very similar, there are some easily recognisable characteristics which help distinguish them. The young branches of *Erica arborea*, or the "Heather Tree", are white and tomentose with leaves at the most 8 millimetres long and white to pinkish flowers; the branches of *Erica scoparia* are hairless and the bark flakes off longitudinally, the leaves can reach 15 millimetres in length and the margins are turned inwards, giving the leaf a fleshy look; the flowers are pink to reddish. *E. scoparia* subsp. *platycodon* is endemic to the Macaronesian Islands.

HYPERICUM GLANDULOSUM AIT. [71]
(Hypericaceae) Hiperico

A shrub up to one metre tall with thin and slender resinous stems. Often found on the edges of laurel-leaf woodlands. Opposite, ovate-elliptical leaves with glandular hairs on the margins. Golden yellow flowers arranged at the branch tips. The sepals have the same glandular hairs as the leaves. The "Glandular Hiperico" is endemic to the Macaronesian Islands.

ADENOCARPUS FOLIOLOSUS (AIT.) DC. [68]
(Leguminosae) Codeso

A shrub very similar to *A. viscosus*, from which it differs for the lack of glandular hairs, especially on the calyx, which is therefore less viscous. It lives at lower levels, generally below 1,200-1,400 metres, whilst *A. viscosus* is found at higher altitudes.

CYTISUS SCOPARIUS (L.) LINK [69]
(Leguminosae)

Upright shrub whose branches are square in section. Small, trifoliate leaves but simple on younger branches. Large, yellow flowers (25 mm) on the higher branches and in dense inflorescences. The bean is black and thickly covered with hair. Distributed over Europe and recently introduced to the Canary Islands by man. "Broom" also has an ornamental value both for its leaves, the colour of which can vary in the different species of cultivars, and for its flowers.

ULEX EUROPAEUS L. [70]
(Leguminosae)

Although *Ulex europaeus* does not grow in the wild state on the Canary Islands but was recently introduced by man, it grows extremely well in its new environment and has thus become part of the plant associations together with Broom. Easily recognised by its many thorns.

68

69

70

71

PINEWOODS

The xerophilous montane vegetation, which develops above the belt affected by the mists brought by the Trade Winds, is dominated by pinewoods of *Pinus canariensis*. The tree line for the Canary pinewoods varies between 1,000 and 2,000 metres, but on the ancient lava flows of the eastern slopes of Teide, Tenerife, some isolated pines can be found as high as 2,400 m altitude. In the lower levels of the pinewood range, which still feel the strong influence of the wet mists, heliophilous shrubs occur, typical of the degradation stages of the laurel-leaf woodlands.

The pinewoods are characterised by the presence of two leguminous shrubs: *Adenocarpus viscosus* and *Chamaecytisus proliferus*, as well as *Lotus hildebrandtii*, a small herbaceous plant, again belonging to the Legume family which can be found in abundance on the south-western slopes of Teide. *Cistus symphytifolius*, *Echium virescens* and *Micromeria varia*, on the other hand, are linked more to the degradation stages of pinewoods covered with less pine trees.

The largest extensions of this type of vegetation are found at: Tenerife, Gran Canaria, La Palma and Hierro. The pinewoods of Tenerife are the favourite habitat of *Fringilla teydea* subsp. *teydea* (Blue Chaffinch) and *Dendrocopos major* subsp. *canariensis* (Teide Great Spotted Woodpecker), whilst the Gran Canaria pinewoods are home to *Fringilla teydea* subsp. *polatzeki* and *D. major* subsp. *thanneri*. This explains the exceptional naturalistic importance of these habitats and justifies their inclusion in the protected areas within the European Community (European Community Directive 43/92).

All the grandeur of Teide and examples of the vegetation with Pinus canariensis.

CHAMAECYTISUS PROLIFERUS (L. FIL.) LINK 73
(Leguminosae) Escobón

Bush branched from the base, up to 4 metres tall, sometimes reaching 7. Trunk with dark grey bark. Trifoliate, greyish green leaves carried on a petiole more or less the same length as the leaves. White flowers borne on the highest portions of the branches. Fruits are pods up to 7 centimetres long. The species is very variable and some varieties have been recognised which do not seem to depend on ecological conditions. *C. proliferus* subsp. *angustifolius* (O.Kuntze) Kunk. seems to be distinct from the typical examples found only at La Palma, whilst *C. proliferus* subsp. *proliferus* occurs on Tenerife, La Gomera and Gran Canaria. The "Escobón" is melliferous and produces excellent honey.

72

PINUS CANARIENSIS CHR.SM. EX DC. 72
(Pinaceae) Pino canario

Can be a large tree (some specimens are known to reach 60 m in height and have a trunk over 2.5 m in diameter). Needle-like leaves, sometimes pale green, reaching 30 centimetres in length and arranged in tufts of three. Straight trunk, bark a grey colour with grey-reddish plates. The "Canary Pine" is endemic to the archipelago, but it only grows wild at Tenerife, La Palma, Gran Canaria and Hierro; reports for La Gomera refer to specimens introduced by man.

73

45

74

75

ADENOCARPUS VISCOSUS (WILLD.) WEBB & BERTH. 74 75
(Leguminosae)
Codeso del Pico

Shrub with very dense branches and leaves, endemic to the Canary Islands (Tenerife and La Palma) where it can easily be found above the tree line. The small, trifoliate and sticky leaves mostly occur in bundles on the younger branches. Yellow flowers on the highest portion of the branches.

LOTUS CAMPYLOCLADUS WEBB & BERTH. 76
(Leguminosae) Corazoncillo

Endemic species to the Island of Tenerife where it is easily found among the underbrush of sparse pinewoods, especially on the western slopes of Teide. The yellow flowers of this rather small, creeping herbaceous plant, make a striking contrast to the grey of the volcanic lava.

CISTUS SYMPHYTIFOLIUS LAM. 77
(Cistaceae) Amagante

Easily recognised for the deep pink colour and size of its flowers, which can reach 5 centimetres in diameter, but the flowers of this cistus are extremely delicate and are easily damaged by a storm. Shrub reaching a metre in height with opposite, velvet-like leaves with prominent veins. Very common in the lower part of the altitudinal belt corresponding to pinewoods. An endemic to the Canary Islands.

78

ECHIUM VIRESCENS **DC.** [78]
(Boraginaceae)

Highly branched shrub up to
2 metres high. Lanceolate leaves,
long and tapered, flat and hispid
due to sparse, short and rigid hairs.
Flowers vary from pink to pale blue
and are arranged in dense clusters
at the branch tips.

MICROMERIA VARIA
BENTHAM [79]
(Labiatae) Tomillo común

Small prostrate shrub with more or
less compact branches nearly always
thickly pubescent, especially the
younger branches. Leaves usually
opposite, sometimes in small
bunches, linear or slightly lanceolate
with the margins folding upwards.
White-to-pink flowers arranged in
verticils. Endemic to the Canary
Islands.

79

THE HIGHLANDS

Above the 2,300 metre mark, the limit for the development of forest vegetation, the real and proper "highland habitat" takes over. This type of habitat is characterised by hot, dry summers and very cold winters, with frequent frosts from October to April. This type of habitat is only found at Cumbres de Garafia, La Palma and on Teide, and it is this last locality that can boast the greatest development both in terms of extension and variety of species, many of which are endemic and rare. Most of these plants exhibit characteristic adaptations to life in a habitat with low rainfall and strong insolation, for example the reduced size of their aerial parts protected with a thick, woolly silver-white covering. These high mountain coenoses are dominated by shrub and low-shrub Leguminosae, among which *Spartocytisus supranubianus* lends a typical aspect to the landscape.

Other shrubs and herbs of particular interest in these areas are: *Descurainia bourgeauana*, *Erysimum scoparium*, *Scrophularia glabrata*, *Pterocephalus lasiospermus* and *Nepeta teydea*. In the more rocky areas, *Echium wildpretii* can be found, a huge borage which morphologically strongly resembles the giant herbaceous plants of the mountains of Central Africa, especially the tree-like Senecios and giant Lobelias.

On the more recent lava slopes the white flowers of *Argyranthemum teneriffae* (the Teide daisy) stand out. Still higher, over the 2,500 metres mark, can be found *Viola cheirantifolia* (the Teide violet) with its splendid violet flowers, whose population over the last twenty years has dwindled due to the construction of a cable car to the top of the volcano, which has led to the increased presence of man.

The lava fields of Teide are an interesting habitat for the protection of nature within the European Community (European Community Directive 43/92).

Three spendid views of Teide.

SPARTOCYTISUS SUPRANUBIANUS (L. FIL.) SANTOS [80]
(Leguminosae) Retama del Pico

This species dominates the high areas of the Canary mountains. A shrub between 2 and 4 metres high, with round, wide, uniform head on a small trunk. The branches are rush-like, slightly grooved. Leaves small and trifoliate, maximum 2 centimetres. White or slightly pink flowers highly perfumed covering practically all the upper half of the stems. Fruits black when ripe. Melliferous plant.

80

DESCURAINIA BOURGEAUANA (FOURN.) WEBB EX O.E.SCHULZ [81]
(Cruciferae) Hierba pajonera

Woody shrub with erect herbaceous stem up to a metre tall. Leaves deeply pinnate, with linear leaflets. Flowers with four yellow petals arranged in groups at the tip of the small branches. A species endemic to the highest peaks of the Teide, common over 2,000 metres.

ERYSIMUM SCOPARIUM (BROUSS. EX WILLD.) WETTST. [82]
(Cruciferae) Alhelí del Teide

Small shrub with erect stem, woody in the lower portion and herbaceous in the upper. Leaves greyish on account of the thick covering of hairs. Flowers a violet colour varying in intensity. This plant, which is quite common on Tenerife and Gran Canaria between 1,800 and 2,200 metres, is difficult to tell from *E. virescens* (Webb ex Christ.) Wettst. which is found on all the islands but at lower altitudes, generally below 1,000 metres. The only safe characteristic which allows them to be distinguished are the hairs, in *E. scoparius* they are not branched whilst in *E. virescens* they branch into three.

81↑ 82↓

83

ECHIUM WILDPRETII
PEARS. EX HOOK. FIL. 84
(Boraginaceae) Taginaste rojo

One of the most beautiful plants which grow in the highest areas of the Canary Islands, and can be found on the Teide, at Tenerife and at El Paso, at La Palma. A giant borage with linear-lanceolate, hispid, ashy green leaves up to 40 centimetres long, arranged in a rosette close to the ground. At maturity, a long leafy spike grows from the middle of the rosette reaching up to 2 metres in height. The bright red flowers are borne on the upper half of the spike and are protected by a leafy bract.

84

SCROPHULARIA GLABRATA
AIT. 83
(Scrophulariaceae) Hierba de cumbre

Small shrub with very leafy, herbaceous branches. Leaves whole. The small flowers, along the upper portion of the branches, are purple or dark red. *S. glabrata* is endemic to the higher areas of the Canary Islands and occurs on Tenerife and La Palma.

PTEROCEPHALUS LASIOSPERMUS
LINK EX BUCH 85
(Dipsacaceae)

An endemic species limited exclusively to the island of Tenerife. A shrub which can grow up to one metre tall, with branches and leaves thickly covered with silvery-white hairs. Flowers pink of varying intensity arranged in small, compact inflorescences at the tips of the highest branches.

85

51

NEPETA TEYDEA WEBB & BERTH. [86]
(Labiatae)

Like most of the plants which live in this type of habitat, the "Teide Nepeta" is only found on Tenerife and La Palma. *N. teydea* is a perennial herb of the Thyme family, thickly covered with dense hair, the scape can reach a metre and a half in height. Leaves opposite with toothed edges. Flowers pale blue to whitish, arranged in a generally branched, spiked inflorescence.

ARGYRANTHEMUM TENERIFFAE HUMPHR. [87]
(Compositae)
Margarita del Teide

Small, prostrate shrub growing on the lava flows from the last volcanic eruptions on Teide. The white flowers are easily seen against the contrasting dark substrate.
A. teneriffae is endemic to this area.

86↑ 87↓

CLIFFS AND ROCKS

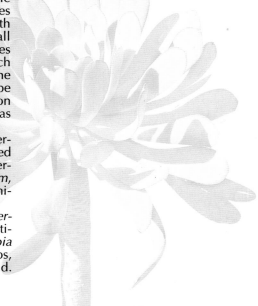

The rocky terrain of the Canary Islands highlands has given rise to a rock plant community characterised by a high number of endemic species, some of which are limited to extremely small areas. Species of the genera *Aeonium* and *Grenowia* are typical of this coenosis, both belonging to the *Crassulacea* family (the Stonecrops). These are small bushes or perennial non-woody plants, often with succulent leaves arranged in a basal rosette attached to the perpendicular cliff faces, which remain there the whole year through. When they reach maturity, the scape bearing the flowers grows from the rosettes; this can sometimes be very long and droops from the cliff walls. The rocky community grows on natural rocks as well as on artificial buildings, especially walls, as long as they are not cement.

On the wet and shady slopes of the Anaga massif, to the North of Tenerife and within the laurel-leaf woodland belt, a coenosis has developed characterised by *Aeonium cuneatum*, an endemism found only on Tenerife, *A. ciliatum* and *Aichrysum laxum. Aeonium haworthii, A. urbicum, Sonchus acaulis* and *S. congestus* can be found in the hotter and drier microclimates

In very wet crevices on the Teno massif, which feel the sea winds, *Vieraea laevigata, Crambe scaberrima* and *Cheirolophus canariensis* constitute an aerohaline community, which can reach as far as the *Euphorbia aphylla* coenosis, whilst on artificial substrates like walls and roof tops, species like *Antirrhinum majus* and *Centranthus ruber* can often be found.

A rocky meadow with Sonchus *in flower.*

AEONIUM CUNEATUM
WEBB & BERTH. [88]
(Crassulaceae) Bejeque

The genus *Aeonium* consists of over 30 species, mostly distributed in the Macaronesian Islands with some representatives in Morocco and Yemen. It includes perennial herbaceous plants, with a woody basal portion and succulent, generally wedge-shaped leaves arranged in a basal rosette, rarely along the stem. Flowers small, but arranged in sometimes very large

88

inflorescences which are erect and shaped like a pyramid. *A. cuneatum* has a very short, erect stem and almost always bears runners. The basal rosette can reach 50 centimetres in diameter and is composed of glabrous, whitish to pale blue leaves. Pale yellow flowers arranged in a cone-shaped inflorescence, up to a metre long and 30 centimetres wide at the base. Endemic to Tenerife.

AEONIUM CILIATUM
(WILLD.) WEBB & BERTH. [89]
(Crassulaceae) Bejeque

Differs from *A. cuneatum* on account of its more developed and branched woody base. The rosettes are smaller (not exceeding 20 centimetres in diameter), a deep green colour and often reddish at the edges. Flowers can be white to green or slightly pinkish. The inflorescence is pyramidal, very branched but smaller than in the previous species. Only found at Tenerife and La Palma.

AICHRYSUM LAXUM
(HAW.) BRAMW. [90]
(Crassulaceae)

Erect, slightly hairy annual or biennial. Stem up to 30 centimetres high with more or less erect branches. Leaves fleshy, hairy to woolly and almost rhomboid. Flowers yellow, arranged in loose, sparse inflorescences. Species endemic to the Canary Islands but not found on Lanzarote or Fuerteventura.

89↑ 90↓

91

AEONIUM URBICUM (CHR. SM. EX BUCH) WEBB & BERTH. [92][93]
(Crassulaceae) Bejeque

The largest species of the genus *Aeonium*. Branched shrub up to 2 metres high. Glaucous leaves arranged in a rosette no wider than 35 centimetres in diameter. More or less variegated pink flowers, arranged in inflorescences up to 75 centimetres long and 45 centimetres wide. Endemic to Tenerife and La Gomera.

92

SONCHUS ACAULIS DUM.-COURS. [94]
(Compositae) Cerraja

Perennial herbaceous plant with woody base. Leaves organised in a large basal rosette which can reach up to a metre in diameter. Tomentose, pinnate leaves with sharp tip. Floral scape can reach a metre and a half in height; the composite inflorescences carried at the top are characteristic because they are sheathed by white, hairy bracts. Species endemic to the Canary Islands.

93

AEONIUM HAWORTHII SALM.-DYKE EX WEBB & BERTH. [91]
(Crassulaceae) Bejeque

A. haworthii is characterised by rosettes reaching a maximum diameter of 11 centimetres. Pale pink or white flowers streaked with pink. In this case the inflorescence is roundish with a diameter no greater than 20 centimetres.
Endemic to Tenerife.

94

SONCHUS RADICATUS
AIT. [95]
(Compositae) Cerraja

Differs from the former species for its usually less tomentose, fewer but larger composite inflorescences. Endemic to Tenerife.

VIERAEA LAEVIGATA
(BROUSS. EX WILLD.) WEBB [96]
(Compositae) Amargosa

This lives only on the basalt slopes flanking the road nears the Fraele rocks, near the Teno massif, i.e. the north-western part of the Island of Tenerife. *Vieraea laevigata* is associated with rocky ground and characterised by flowers clustered in yellow composite inflorescences. The stem is greyish. Leaves ovate-lanceolate, with minutely toothed edges especially towards the tip. It flowers in spring and its yellow flowers liven up the dark grey basalt, adding even more colour to this already beautiful area. Extremely rare species, and new roads and construction of canals for water collection are unfortunately reducing the population even more.

95↑ 96↓

CRAMBE SCABERRIMA
WEBB EX BRAMW. [97]
(Cruciferae) Col del Risco

Shrub reaching a maximum height of one and a half metres. Ovate, very rough leaves to touch, with slightly dentate edges, with very short petiole which expands into two wings. Small, white flowers, arranged in loose inflorescences. The species is endemic to Tenerife and abundant especially in the Teno area where *C. laevigata* also occurs, the latter endemic limited to this area. This differs from *C. scaberrima* on account of its smooth leaves, smaller size and is in danger of extinction.

97

CHEIROLOPHUS CANARIENSIS (BROUSS. EX WILLD.) HOLUB [98]
(Compositae) Abrojo

A rare species, endemic to the Island of Tenerife. It is possible to find it along the high rocky coasts at Fraele, at Cape Bellavista. A species which grows on the basalt slopes, which it contrasts thanks to its pale mauve composite inflorescences. The leaves of the "Fiordelise" are pinnate-lobate; the lobes are sometimes so unmarked that the leaf may appear to be whole.

ANTIRRHINUM MAJUS L. [99]
(Scrophulariaceae)
Boca del Dragón

Certainly the most common of the species of this genus and grown for centuries in gardens all over the world. The "Greater Snap-Dragon" is a perennial herbaceous plant up to 75 centimetres high, which prefers sunny and rocky substrates,

99

especially if on a slope like dry walls. The brightly coloured and variegated flowers, from white to yellow with purple streaks to dark purple, reach 5 centimetres in length. There are many cultivars of *A. majus* on account of its long scape and for the variety of the flowers.

CENTRANTHUS RUBER (L.) DC. [100]
(Valerianaceae) Hierba de San Jorge

Often associated with the Snap-Dragon, with which it shares its preference for the dry walls found in the country or rock gardens in town. The stem of the "Red Valerian" can be up to 80 centimetres high, generally branched, with opposite glaucous leaves. Purple or reddish, small flowers clustered in rich umbrella shaped inflorescences. Both the leaves and the flowers make *C. ruber* a very decorative plant. It comes from the regions surrounding the Mediterranean Sea from Asia Minor to Morocco.

100

CULTIVATED AREAS AND WASTELAND

A mong the different vegetation belts, some communities can be found growing in areas where agriculture has been abandoned or at the edges of areas affected by human activity. In other words these communities are found where organic substances have tended to accumulate thus tending to increase the amount of nitrates in the soil.

Some species often found on abandoned and stony ground are *Ricinus communis, Nicotiana glauca* and *Rumex lunaria*, species of neotropical origin such as *Tropaeolum majus*, the Prickly Pears (*Opuntia dillenii, O. ficus-barbarica*) and *Ageratina adenophora*, now naturalised not only in the Canary Islands Archipelago but also most of the Mediterranean.

Alongside the former communities, dominated by low or high forms of shrubs, but still under the same ecological conditions, other coenoses occur dominated by non-woody perennials and grasses such as *Pennisetum setaceum, Psoralea bituminosa, Achyranthes aspera* and *Glaucium corniculatum*, especially common along the edges of the roads and in strongly disturbed areas. *Oxalis pes-caprae* and *Carpobrotus edulis* can also be added to this list, species imported by man as ornamental plants from South Africa and Central America respectively.

Among the annual species, *Mesembryanthemum crystallinum* and *M. nodiflorum* can be mentioned, two prostrate, succulent species originally from South Africa which have become naturalised in many hot and dry regions of the world. Both species vegetate between autumn and winter, forming multi-coloured carpets on the rocky substrates near the sea.

In the abandoned agricultural areas, especially if herbicides were not used in excess, *Echium plantagineum, Sisymbrium officinalis, Asphodelus aestivus* and *Scrophularia arguta* can be found.

Meadows with Echium plantagineum *and* Sisymbrium officinalis *at Las Mercedes, Island of Tenerife.*

RICINUS COMMUNIS L. [101] [102]
(Euphorbiaceae)
Higuera infernal

The "Castor-Oil Plant" is a species which belongs to the *Euphorbiaceae* family, even though it does not look like one. A plant with herbaceous stems which can reach 12 metres in height, but which does not generally exceed 4. Leaves palmate up to 60 centimetres in diameter whose colour can vary from various intensities of green to purple. Flowers arranged in clusters at the tip of the stem; the female flowers are concentrated on lower portion of the inflorescence whilst the male flowers occur at the tip. This plant grows wild in North-east Africa and the Middle East but has spread to the whole of the Mediterranean Basin reaching Europe and the Canary Islands. Many cultivars have been created by man for the different types of variegated leaves. The plant is grown for its oil obtained from the seeds even though the cuticle of these contains ricinus, a highly toxic substance, which even at low doses is considered one of the most poisonous substances found in nature.

101

NICOTIANA GLAUCA GRAHAM. [105]
(Solanaceae) Bobo

The "Tobacco Tree" reaches 7-8 metres in height, with a flexible stem and glaucous, smooth leaves borne on a petiole. Pale yellow flowers arranged in panicles at the tips of the small branches. Curiously also called the "Mustard Tree", this plant originally came from South America but has become naturalised in the hot dry areas of North Africa and the Canary Islands. Like all the species of the genus *Nicotiana*, it contains an alkaloid (nicotine) which gives it toxic properties.

102

RUMEX LUNARIA L. [103]
(Polygonaceae)
Vinagrera

The only species belongin[g] genus *Rumex* to be found Canary Islands, to which i[s] endemic. *R. lunaria* is a sh[rub] the Dock family) with pale s[tems] and flexible branches which i[s] easily recognised on account [o]f its round-ovate leaves.

TROPAEOLUM MAJUS L. [104] [106]
(Tropaeolaceae) Capuchino

The "Indian Watercress" or "Garden Nasturtium" is a herbaceous plant with long stems creeping on the ground. Can be immediately recognised on ruins and waste land by the roadside for its beautiful bright flowers, varying in colour from orange, deep yellow to brownish red. Unlike the "Castor-Oil Plant", all its parts are edible and the seeds can be used instead of capers. Like true Nasturtiums, which really belong the *Cruciferae* family, the "Indian Watercress" can be used to obtain mustard oil. Originally from South America (Columbia, Peru and Bolivia) it has been imported to Europe since 1684. Today it is grown almost all over the world as a decorative plant with very many cultivars.

103

104

107

OPUNTIA FICUS-BARBARICA A. BERGER [107][108]
(Cactaceae) Tunera
OPUNTIA DILLENII (KER-GAWL.) HAW. [109]
(Cactaceae) Maleza

The genus *Opuntia* includes all those plants which are generally called "Prickly Pears". In actual fact the genus comprises over 200 species, all originally from the American continent, from Canada to Patagonia. They are shrubs or small trees with the trunk consisting of rounded, generally flattened segments, the leaves of which have been transformed into tufts of soft to hard spikes. Many species of the genus *Opuntia* are grown in hot and dry areas all over the world and there are numerous cultivars. In the hot-dry areas of the Canary Islands, two kinds of "Prickly Pears" can be found, both growing wild. They can be distinguished from each other by their spikes: *O. dillenii* has long, rigid spines in groups of three whilst *O. ficus-barbarica* has short, fine spines arranged in more numerous groups. It is easy to tell them apart when they are in flower: *O. dillenii* has yellow flowers whilst the other has reddish flowers. Both originally came from Mexico.

108

109

AGERATINA ADENOPHORA (SPRENG.) KING & ROBINS. 110
(Compositae)

Small shrub up to a metre and a half tall with flexible stems covered with glandular hairs. Opposite, oval leaves with pointed tip, usually pubescent on the lower page. Composite inflorescences whitish. Originally from Mexico but it has become naturalised and grows wild.

PENNISETUM SETACEUM (FORSSK.) CHIOV. 111
(Graminaceae) Cerillo

Along the main roads of the Islands can often be seen a tall grass growing up to a metre in height, characterised by its thick tufts and feathery pink-purple ears. Close up, it strongly resembles one of the tall grasses of the African savannahs. Its appearance has made it a valuable decorative plant and for this reason several cultivars exist. *P. setaceum* is distributed in the hot areas of Africa and in the Canary Islands it can be considered as a naturalised species.

110

111

112

PSORALEA BITUMINOSA **L.** 112
(Leguminosae) Tedera

Perennial herbaceous plant reaching a metre in height, whose trifoliate leaves are born on a petiole up to 8 centimetres long. Deep purple flowers gathered in hemispheric inflorescences. Although *Psoralea* is quite easy to recognise, any doubts can be eliminated by simply rubbing it to release its characteristic smell of bitumen, which makes it unmistakable.

113

ACHYRANTHES ASPERA **L.** 113
(Amaranthaceae) Malpica

Small shrub up to 50-80 centimetres tall with upright leafy branches, thickly pubescent and tetragonal in the upper portion. Fairly small leaves (2.5 x 3.5 centimetres maximum), deep green on upper blade and whitish on lower due to the thick down. Pale pink flowers arranged in long inflorescences at the tips of the stems.

ESCHSCHOLZIA CALIFORNICA **CHAM.** 114
(Papaveraceae)

Annual with tendency to becoming a perennial, no more than 60 centimetres tall. Leaves glaucous, finely pubescent or smooth. Flowers with four yellow or pale orange petals. The fruit is up to 8 centimetres long. Originally from California, the species has been widely grown all over the world in areas with a hot-wet climate, where it tends to grow wild and become invasive. Numerous cultivars of *E. californica* have been produced for their variegated flowers ranging from pale yellow to white to orange-red.

114↑

115

116

OXALIS PES-CAPRAE L. [115]
(Oxalidaceae) Trebonilla

The genus *Oxalis* comprises species which are now cosmopolitan, although it is reported as originally coming from South Africa and South America. The "Bermuda Four-leafed Clover" has long been used as a decorative plant in many regions, especially in hot-dry areas. *Oxalis* is a herbaceous bulbous plant with quadrifoliate leaves carried on petioles up to 12 centimetres long. Flowers bright yellow borne on long pedunculate umbrellas.

CARPOBROTUS EDULIS (L.) L.BOLUS [116]
(Aizoaceae) Balsamo

The "Hottentot Fig" is also a species originally from South Africa which has become naturalised in many regions of the world especially those with a hot-dry season (Australia, California and Southern Europe). A herbaceous creeping plant characterised by its fleshy, edible leaves. Opposite, thick triangular and keeled leaves up to 8-12 centimetres long. Flowers can be yellow or purple and reach 5-6 centimetres in diameter.

117

MESEMBRYANTHEMUM CRYSTALLINUM L. [117]
(Aizoaceae) Barilla

The genus originally came from Namibia, but most of the species have spread all over the world especially in those countries bordering the sea with a hot climate. The "Firefly Plant" is an annual with stems creeping on the ground, succulent ovate-spatulate leaves covered with very many small papillae. The whitish or pink flowers, 2-3 centimetres in diameter, only open when illuminated directly by the sun.

MESEMBRYANTHEMUM NODIFLORUM L. [118]
(Aizoaceae) Algazul

Very similar to the previous species with which it shares the same habitat. Can be recognised from the former by its narrower (2-3 millimetres thick), linear, semi-cylindrical leaves covered with larger papillae.

118

119

120

121↑ 123↓

122

ECHIUM PLANTAGINEUM L. [119]

(Boraginaceae)
Taginaste

Herbaceous annual covered with hispid, blackish, glandular hairs. Undivided, lanceolate or ovate leaves, the basal leaves larger than those borne on the stem. Flowers, up to 3.5 centimetres long, are pale blue and arranged in branched, long inflorescences. *E. plantagineum* is a very common plant in cultivated areas all over South Europe.

SISYMBRIUM OFFICINALIS (L.) SCOP. [120]

(Cruciferae) Aramago

Annual non-woody plant, of the Crucifer or Cabbage Family, up to 80 centimetres tall, erect stem, rough to the touch on account of the numerous prickly hairs, reddish in colour tending to violet. Leaves pinnate, flowers yellow with petals not exceeding 2 millimetres in length, arranged in long, linear inflorescences.

SCROPHULARIA ARGUTA SOL. EX AIT. [121] [122]

(Scrophulariaceae)

Annual figwort up to 25 centimetres high characterised by its tetragonal stem. Leaves ovate with toothed edges. Flowers small and purple coloured arranged in spiked inflorescences.

ASPHODELUS AESTIVUS BROT. [123]

(Asphodelaceae)
Cebolla de culebra

The genus *Asphodelus* comprises herbaceous plants with flat leaves up to 60 centimetres long which are arranged in a basal rosette. On reaching maturity, an erect stem grows from the centre of the rosette which may be branched at the top bearing the flowers. In this species the stem is strong reaching 2 metres in height and the often numerous flowers are whitish.

TOWNS AND GARDENS

The distribution of the ecosystems described so far depends on one or more natural factors affecting them, such as light, temperature, humidity and type of substrate, all of which determine the limits of development for living things. These habitats can be defined as "naturally determined". On the other hand, gardens, flower beds and parks are made wherever man pleases and on criteria based on the culture and level of civilisation of a people. Thus, species which have different needs from those of their new environment can be found growing together, but which are kept alive by the constant attention of man. This type of habitat can be defined as "anthropically determined".

The union of the Canary Islands to the Spanish Crown during a period of intense traffic with its South American Colonies, and their position along the main shipping routes between South American and Europe, allowed many tropical species to be introduced, which became well adapted to their new, hot wet climate. The decorative plants found in the parks and gardens of the Canary Islands do not come from South America alone, but also from Australia, South Africa, India and South-west Asia and Madagascar.

Left: an example of **Spathodea campanulata;** *below: balconies in flower at Puerto de la Cruz, Tenerife.*

Many of these plants make the parks, streets and gardens very pleasant with their colours and sweet perfumes, but it should always be remembered that the introduction of exotic plants is always a sort of environmental contamination because one given area may not always be capable of integrating the new species. Some species carry parasites from their original countries, which, under new ecological conditions, may cause infestations which are difficult to control and may seriously damage the local ecosystems. Again, these plants may be resistant to local parasites and increase in number undisturbed to the point of replacing the local flora.

If exotic flora is to continue to make our lives more pleasant without damaging the local natural heritage, man must be able to regulate his intervention by limiting the use of these plants exclusively to artificial environments, where nature has long given way to infrastructures. The species described in this section are given in alphabetical order, according to their scientific name.

Decorative garden beds and an avenue lined with **Jacaranda mimosifolia** *trees at Puerto de la Cruz.*

124

126

125

ACALYPHA WILKENSIANA *MULL.ARG.* 124 125
(Euphorbiaceae)

Evergreen shrub originally from Malaysia, about 4.5 m high. Leaves simple, elliptic, about 20 centimetres long, bronzed green in colour with copper to purple hues. Flowers very small, clustered in spiked inflorescence

up to 10 centimetres long. Grown for the splashes of colour it gives to flower beds and hedge rows.

ACOKANTHERA OBLONGIFOLIA *(HOCHST.) CODD.* 127
(Apocynaceae)

An evergreen shrub, originally from South Africa. It can reach 7 metres in height. Leaves opposite, elliptic, leathery, glossy and about 12 centimetres long. Blooms from autumn to spring and the flowers, up to 2 centimetres across, are white and clustered in dense inflorescences at the tip of the branches and smell very like jasmine. The fruits are beautiful deep purple coloured globular berries. All parts of the plant are highly poisonous and were once used by the local people to poison their arrows. Has medicinal properties.

AECHMEA DISTHICANTHA *LEM.* 126
(Bromeliaceae)

This herbaceous plant can reach 60 centimetres in height, with narrow leaves imbricated in a very compact basal rosette. Leaves erect with the proximal portion expanded in a triangle and narrow distal portion ending in a spike. The pink floral scape can grow up to a metre tall and bears numerous flowers supported by bracts equipped with short thorns. Flowers small, purple or blue. Originally from South Brazil and Uruguay.

127

128

129

130

plant with leaves arranged in a basal rosette, up to a metre long, whose colour can vary from a more or less brilliant green to reddish with spiked teeth along the margins. A flowering scape grows from the basal rosette, usually 50 centimetres high, with an inflorescence at the tip consisting of many red to violet flowers. The fruit is very characteristic and consists of numerous single fruits, up to 200, fused together with a tuft of spiny leaves at the tip. The fruits of the "Honey-Gold" cultivar can weigh as much as 7 kilos. The pineapple originally came from Brazil, but today is grown in all areas with a hot-wet climate.

ALLAMANDA NERIIFOLIA HOOK. 128
(Apocynaceae)

Evergreen shrub, up to a metre and a half high, with woody branches at the basal portion. Leaves up to 15 centimetres long, elliptical, sharp tipped and arranged in verticils of 2 to 5 leaves. Flowers funnel shaped, yellow with yellow-red striations and clustered in loose inflorescences. A garden pot plant and used to cover walls and palisades.

ALPINIA ZERUMBET (PERS.) B.L.BURTT & R.M.SM. 131
(Zingiberaceae)

A perennial grass with an underground rhizome from which numerous aerial branches leave reaching 3.5 metres in height. Leaves lanceolate, with the widened portion up to 75 centimetres long and 15 centimetres wide, sheathed petiole and pubescent edges. Flowers trilobed arranged in drooping terminal panicles, white streaked with pink. Flowers the whole year through and for this reason is much used in floriculture. Originally from South-east Asia.

ANANAS COMOSUS (L.) MERR 129
(Bromeliaceae)

The "Pineapple" is a plant much exploited by man, as its fruits can be eaten directly or processed for the food industry; moreover the fruits yield a proteolitic enzyme similar to pancreatic juices. It is also cultivated as an ornamental plant for its leaves and flowers and many cultivars have been produced. A perennial herbaceous

APTENIA CORDIFOLIA (L. FIL.) N.E.BR. 130
(Aizoaceae)

Small, creeping shrub no more than 50 centimetres high. Leaves opposite, rather fleshy with short petiole and sharp tip. It is covered with minute papillae. Flowers purple, either single or clustered in groups of 3 to 4. Originally from South Africa and grown as an ornamental species especially in areas near the sea.

BAUHINIA VARIEGATA L. [132]
(Leguminosae)

Deciduous tree, up to 10 metres high, originally from India. Characterised by a very large but not compact head of foliage. Leaves paripinnate, composed, with lanceolate leaflets. Called the "Orchid Tree" for its very beautiful flowers, up to 12 cm in diameter and magenta in colour, streaked with purple and white and clustered in lateral inflorescences at the tips of the short branches. Several cultivars exist of this highly decorative plant which differ for the variegation of the flowers. The particular shape of the foliage makes this tree very suitable for bordering the roads, also because, like most of the *Leguminosae*, it grows very quickly and does not have particular needs regarding the type of soil. It is used in the dying industry for its high

132

content of tannin in the bark; in India the flowers and leaves are eaten.

BOUGANVILLEA X BUTTIANA HOLTT. & STAND. [133]
(Nyctaginaceae)

An evergreen, woody climbing plant with thorns along the stem. Leaves sharp, glabrous, up to 20 centimetres long, with the lower blade paler than the upper. Small flowers, hardly visible, their vexillary function substituted by the purple coloured calyx and three bracts of the same colour and shaped like the leaves. Flowers all year through and grows quickly; for this reason it has long been grown as a decorative plant and several cultivars exist.

133↑ 134↓

BROUGMASIA VERSICOLOR LAGERTH [134]
(Solanaceae)

Evergreen tree up to 5 metres high, originally from Ecuador. Leaves elliptical with sharp tips, can vary from glabrous to pubescent and reach 60 centimetres in length. Flowers pendulous and ranging from salmon pink to pale peach, up to

17 centimetres long with a funnel shaped corolla, giving them the name "Angel's Trumpet". The fruit is a characteristic fusiform bean up to 21 centimetres long. All parts of the plant are poisonous as it contains a toxic alkaloid which, if administered in low doses, can be used as a weak narcotic. Flowers the whole year through, is very resistant and requires little care, so is much used in parks and gardens.

135

136

CALLISTEMON VIMINALIS R.Br. 135 136
(Myrtaceae)

The name means "plant of the beautiful stamens", a characteristic common to many *Myrtaceae*. A small "Bottle-brush" tree up to 5-6 metres high, with thick head of foliage but with bending branches which gives it its specific name of "viminalis", i.e. similar to those of the wicker willows. The young branches have silky hairs. Leaves alternate, lanceolate. Flowers small, arranged in spiked inflorescence, pale red in colour. Their identification can be difficult, since species of the genus *Callistemon* tend to hybridise. This characteristic has been exploited to produce numerous cultivars. Originally from Australia.

CANNA INDICA L. 137
(Cannaceae)

The genus *Canna* comprises 9 species of rhyzomed perennial herbs, up to 5 metres high, much employed to decorate gardens and to give them an exotic touch. They are all characterised by very long leaves, up to a metre long, whose blades extend into the petiole which in turn extends to form a false stem. The flowers, generally large and of different colours, are arranged in

137↑ 138↓

terminal inflorescences.
The "Indian Hemp" grows up
to 2 metres in height, its large
leaves reaching up to
50 x 20 centimetres, sometimes
veined with purple. The flowers,
single or in pairs, are red but can
range from pink to pale orange,
with the bottom petal sometimes
streaked with yellow. Originally
from Central America but grown
in all regions with a hot wet
climate. There are many cultivars
of *Canna indica* aimed at
increasing the great variety of the
colours of the flowers.

CANNA GLAUCA L. 139
(Cannaceae)

This plant is generally smaller
than *C. indica*, from which it
differs for the slightly smaller
flowers and softer colour tending
towards pale yellow. Like "Indian
Hemp" and all the *Cannaceae*, it
can only be found growing wild
in Central America.

CARICA PAPAYA L. 138
(Caricaceae)

The "Papaya" is a tree reaching
4-8 metres in height. The
palmate-lobate leaves reach up
to 60 centimetres in diameter.
The plant is dioic, the male
flowers are pink or pale yellow
and arranged in drooping
panicles up to 75 centimetres
long, whilst the female flowers
are yellow. The plant is grown for
its edible fruits, similar to melons,
and are yellow or red-orange in
colour. They can be picked for
sale on the market or used in the
pharmaceutical industry to obtain
the digestive alkaloid: papaina.
The Papaya originally came from
the tropical Americas.

140

141

142

143

CASSIA DIDYMOBOTRYA FRESEN. 140
(Leguminosae)

A shrub up to 3 metres high. The leaves, up to 40 centimetres long, are persistent, composite, paripennate and consist of ovate-elliptic leaflets with mucronated tip. The bright yellow flowers are arranged in erect inflorescences reaching up to 30 centimetres in length, at the tip of a long, bowed peduncle. The "Candle Bush" is originally from tropical Africa and is widely used as an ornamental shrub in tropical and subtropical gardens for the colourful effect of its flowers.

CESTRUM AURANTIACUM LINDL. 143
(Solanaceae)

A climbing shrub or small tree up to 6 metres high. Originally from Guatemala. Leaves everlasting, ovate-lanceolate reaching 15 centimetres in length. Flowers yellow and arranged in drooping panicles.

CESTRUM PARQUI L'HER. 141
(Solanaceae)

This species differs from the other *Cestrum* on account of its upright and bushy appearance and for its pale yellow to greenish flowers. Originally from Chile.

CHAMAEROPS HUMILIS L. 142
(Palmae)

One of the smallest living species of palm. It grows wild in the countries bordering the Mediterranean Sea but is cultivated in almost all hot areas. The trunk is short and stumpy, rarely over 4 metres tall. The leaves, arranged at the top of the trunk, are palmate and the widest part is borne on a long petiole. The leaflets of the leaves are leathery with a cutting edge, reaching 30-40 centimetres in length. A highly decorative plant especially if used in open spaces standing on its own.

144

CHLOROPHYTON COMOSUM (THUNB.) JAQUES 144
(Anthericaceae)

Genus with tropical and
subtropical distribution reaching
its maximum diversification of
forms in Southern Africa, from
where it originally comes.
A herbaceous plant with rhizome
and everlasting, fleshy, linear
leaves, characteristically pale
green streaked with white which
gives it its ornamental
appearance. There are very many
cultivars of this plant with
differently variegated leaves.

CLIVIA
X CYRTANTHIFLORA
(VAN HOUTTE) WITTM. 145
(Amaryllidaceae)

Perennial grass with beautiful
bright green leaves arranged in a
dense basal rosette. Leaves thick,

145

up to 90 centimetres long
and 5 centimetres wide.
Flowers carried on a long
petiole growing from the
centre of the rosette.
Flowers funnel shaped and
up to 5 centimetres long,
red to orange in colour and
arranged in a drooping
panicle. Flowers the whole
year through. This plant is
an artificial hybrid
obtained from *C. miniata*
and *C. nobilis*.

146

147

***CLIVIA MINIATA* REGEL** 146
(Amaryllidaceae)

Originally from Southern Africa, this plant differs from *C. cyrtantiflora* for its smaller, darker and more robust leaves and for its upright, larger flowers (7.5 centimetres long). Flowers from spring to the beginning of summer.

***COCCOLOBA UVIFERA* (L.) L.** 147
(Polygonaceae) Uva del mar

The "Sea Grape" is generally a small tree but, in favourable conditions, can reach 15 metres in height. Characteristically large leaves up to 30 centimetres across, leathery, orbicular with marked protruding veins. The highly perfumed flowers are very small but arranged in inflorescences up to 30 centimetres long. Originally from the Antilles, it is mostly employed to line roads, especially near the sea, since it does not have any particular requirements regarding the soil and is resistant to the sea spray and pollutants in general.

CODIAEUM VARIEGATUM BLUME VAR. PICTUM MUELL.ARG. [148] [150]
(Euphorbiaceae)

Evergreen shrub widespread in the Moluccas Islands and Malaysia where it is used by the local people for clothing and as a medicinal plant. It is also employed as a decorative plant thanks to its variegated leaves. These can vary both in size and colouring which goes from green streaked with yellow to dark green streaked with a more or less vivid red.

CORDYLINE STRICTA (SIMS) ENDL. [149]
(Agavaceae)

The genus *Cordyline*, originally from South-east Asia and Australia, comprises very characteristic looking plants on account of the rosette of linear-aciculate leaves arranged on the sometimes branched trunk, growing directly from the ground. The leaves may

148

bear thorns on the margins and tip. When mature, a scape grows from the centre of the rosette reaching up to 4 metres in height and bearing an inflorescence at the tip which, in this species, is highly branched and composed of numerous lilac to pale blue flowers. Several cultivars exist with differently variegated leaves.

149

150

151

CRINUM MOOREI HOOK. 151
(Amaryllidaceae)

A herbaceous perennial, with floral scape up to 1.5 metres high. Leaves basal, linear-lanceolate, up to 125 centimetres long and 15 centimetres wide, generally arched. Very large flowers, reaching 20 centimetres in diameter, white and only rarely streaked with pink. Species originally from South Africa.

ECHINOCACTUS GRUSONII HILDEN. 152
(Cactaceae)

A succulent with globular trunk up to a metre wide. Few but evident ribs separated by deep grooves. The spines, up to 5 centimetres long, are arranged in groups formed of 4 central and golden coloured ones and 10 radial, which are pale yellow to whitish in colour. Flowers yellow to brown. Originally from Mexico.

ENSETE VENTRICOSUM (WELW.) E.E.CHESSM. 153
(Musaceae)

Giant herbaceous plant very similar to the banana (*Musa x paradisiaca*) originally from Central- east Africa and for this reason called the "Abyssinian Banana". The pseudostem or "false stem" can reach 12 metres in height and is thick and robust; leaves arranged at the tip and glacous green with a central, brown vein, reaching up to 6 metres in length. The whitish flowers, completely sheathed in a bract, are arranged in an inflorescence up to 1 metre long. Grown as an ornamental species, several cultivars have been produced.

152

153→

ERYTHRINA CAFFRA THUNB. [156]
(Leguminosae)

This genus, distributed throughout tropical and subtropical regions all over the world, includes some highly valued ornamental species on account of its large flowers arranged in rich, racemose inflorescences. *E. caffra* is a deciduous tree, up to 18-20 metres tall, originally from Southern Africa. The branches are thorny. Leaves composed and imparipinnate. Flowers bright orange, arranged in short drooping inflorescences. Blooms in spring. Several cultivars exist of the species with different coloured flowers. Some species of the genus are pharmacologically important because they contain alkaloids with strong narcotic properties. The seeds are bright red and shiny and are used by the Bantu women to make lucky necklaces. The light wood is used to build canoes.

ERYTHRINA CORALLODENDRON L. [154]
(Leguminosae)

Differs from the former species on account of its bright red flowers arranged in racemes up to 30 centimetres long. The "Coral Tree" is deciduous and reaches 3 metres in height, with the trunk and petioles of the leaves covered with little curved thorns. Leaves pinnate and divided into three leaflets.

154

ESPOSTOA LANATA (KUNTH) BRIT. & ROSE [155]
(Cactaceae)

This succulent, reaching 8 metres in height, has a main stem up to 15 centimetres in diameter, characterised by 20-30 ribs not easily distinguishable because of the thick covering of whitish wool. One or two central, triangular spines which are sharp and up to 2.5 centimetres long, whitish, brown or black. Flowers white or purple which generally open at night. Grows wild in Ecuador and Peru but is widely grown in all arid areas of the world.

155

156

EUPHORBIA MILII DESMOUL. VAR. *SPLENDENS* (BOJER EX HOOK.) URSCH & LEANDRI [157]
(Euphorbiaceae)

Erect plant up to 2 metres high. The stems are succulent and irregularly branched, square or pentangular in section, thorny with straight spines reaching 4 centimetres in length which can become climbing. Sparse leaves, obovate and small (maximum 5 cm long). Flower peduncles reddish. Originally from Madagascar, its long straight spines have given it the name of "Crown of Thorns".

EUPHORBIA PULCHERRIMA WILLD. EX KLOTZSCH. [158]
(Euphorbiaceae)

The "Poinsettia" is probably the best known of all the *Euphorbiaceae*, but it is nevertheless difficult to associate it with *E. canariensis* or *E. balsamifera*. This shrub, with sparse and narrow branches, does not exceed 4 metres in height. Leaves deciduous measuring up to 32 centimetres in length and dark green. The inflorescence shows the same characteristics as all the other *Euphorbiaceae*, in this case the bracts that surround it are identical to the leaves but are a beautiful bright red. Numerous cultivars exist of this species with differently coloured bracts, ranging from red to white. Can be grown as a house pot plant.

FEIJOA SELLOWIANA O.BERG. [159]
(Myrtaceae)

A shrub reaching approximately 6 metres in height characterised by tomentum-covered branches. The leaves are persistent, opposite, bi-coloured with the upper page dark green and the lower tomentose. Single flowers, with purple interior and tomentose exterior. Edible fruits tasting like Pineapple. In the wild it is widespread in Southern Brazil, Paraguay and Argentina.

157

158

159

GAZANIA RIGENS (L.) GAERTN. [160]
(Compositae)

Creeping herbaceous plant, densely covered with leaves which usually have a thick coating of white hair on the under page and, in very young leaves, often on the upper page. Single composite inflorescences at the tip of the short branches, bearing lateral flowers with evident yellow-orange ligules and dark orange central flowers. Species of the genus *Gazania* are used to decorate walls and rock gardens or flowers beds along the road side since they can well tolerate dry conditions and some varieties also tolerate the cold. The genus originally comes from Central South Africa.

GREVILLEA ROBUSTA A.CUNN. [161]
(Proteaceae)

The "Silk Oak" tree originally comes from Australia. In the wild it can

160↑ 161↓

162

reach 30 metres in height but this is rare in cultivated specimens. Leaves everlasting, lanceolate up to 35 centimetres long, white on under side. Flowers a golden yellow, arranged in inflorescences in which they all face upwards. Flowers from spring to summer, when the Grevilleas are spectacular, which is why they are so widely employed as isolated trees in parks and gardens.

HIBISCUS ROSA-SINENSIS L. 162
(Malvaceae)

The genus *Hibiscus* comprises approximately 220 species, including some of the most beautiful decorative plants, all characterised by their splendid flowers. *H. rosa-sinensis* is a shrub up to 4 metres high. Leaves oval, toothed, especially near the tip, about 15 centimetres long. Flowers a more or less deep pink, it flowers the whole year through. The "Rose of China" grows wild over most of tropical and subtropical Asia.

HIBISCUS CALYPHYLLUS CAV. 163
(Malvaceae)

Shares the same morphological characteristics as the previous species but differs from the former for its yellow flowers. Unlike *Hibiscus rosa-sinensis,* which is more common and has numerous cultivars, *H. calyphyllus* is not employed much in horticulture even though it is a wild race which adapts well to cultivation. Originally from tropical and subtropical Africa and thus requiring a hot, wet climate.

163

IPOMOEA ACUMINATA (VAHL) ROEM. & SCHULT. 164
(Convolvulaceae)

Climbing plant originally from tropical America. Leaves can be oval-round or tri-lobate when they are larger, tomentose on the under page. Flowers purple coloured with 10 orange streaks, arranged in inflorescences of a few individuals.

164

IRESINE HERBSTII
HOOK. [165]
(Amaranthaceae)

Herbaceous perennial up to
1.8 metres high characterised by
its bright coloured stem and
leaves. Indeed, the whole plant
is a red-purple colour with more
or less deep streaks.
One cultivar of this species
(*I. herbstii* cv. *aureo-auriculata*)
is totally variegated in different
tones of green. Flowers
insignificant. The wild species
originally comes from South
America.

JACARANDA MIMOSIFOLIA
D.DON [166]
(Bignoniaceae)

Very decorative, medium sized tree
(reaching 15 metres in height) very
suitable for bordering roads and for
parks and gardens. Leaves
composed, paripinnate with 9 pairs
of lanceolate leaflets reaching
80 centimetres in length. Flowers
violet-pale blue arranged in
drooping inflorescences. Flowers
from spring to summer. Originally
from Central and South America.

165

MACKAJA BELLA HARV. 167
(Acanthaceae)

Evergreen shrub up to
2 metres high, originally from
Southern Africa. Leaves
opposite, ovate-oblong with
slightly toothed edges.
Flowers pale pink with darker
venations arranged in
inflorescences at the tips of
the branches. It cannot bear
cold winds, and thus this
plant ideally grows along the
coasts.

MEGASKEPASMA ERYTHROCHLAMYS LINDAU 168
(Acanthaceae)

Shrub reaching 2 metres in height,
originally from Brazil where it is
called the "Red Cape". Leaves
everlasting, oblanceolate up to
30 centimetres long with whole
margins more or less undulating and
a hooked tip. Flowers pale pink or
whitish arranged in a terminal,
spiked inflorescence and supported
by linear, red-purple coloured bracts
up to 4 centimetres long. Blooms
during the winter months and
flowers most in shady sites.

MONSTERA DELICIOSA LIEBM. 169
(Araceae)

Woody climbing plant with
sometimes very long aerial roots.
Generally very large leaves, up to
70 centimetres, deeply laciniated or
with the lobes fused at the edges,
everlasting, coriacious, borne on
petioles which can sometimes
exceed the laminar portion in
length. Flowers arranged in milky-
white spadix inflorescence,
protected by an enlarged spathe of
the same colour. The "Monstera"
originally comes from Central
America.

167

168

169

170

171

172

MUSA X PARADISIACA L. [170] [171] [172]
(Musaceae)

Giant herbaceous perennial up to 8 metres high characterised by a creeping rhizome producing the leaves, which together with the sheaths fuse together to form a pseudostem. The leaves have an up to 2.3 metre long laminar portion, with a marked central reddish vein. Flowers arranged in a reddish, spiked inflorescence protected by a bract. The male flowers are borne high whilst the female flowers are found lower on the plant. The fruits are long beans reaching 9 centimetres in length, or the famous "bananas", grouped together in the well-known "bunch". The genus *Musa* originally comes from South-west Asia but is commonly grown wherever the climate allows. *M. x paradisiaca* is an important alimentary crop and is the staple food in the diets of poorer countries, but it is also a highly decorative plant. Depending on the case, its numerous cultivars thus favour either increased fruit production or the ornamental properties of the plant, producing increasingly more suitable varieties for external decoration.

NERIUM OLEANDER L. [173]
(Apocynaceae)

The Oleander is a shrub reaching 4.5 metres in height. Leaves everlasting, linear-lanceolate up to 25 centimetres long and arranged in verticils of three. Flowers range from pale to deep pink to white. A rustic plant with many cultivars differing in their colour and double petals.

ODONTONEMA CALLISTACHYUM (SCHLECHTEND. & CHAM.) O.KUNTZE [174]
(Acanthaceae)

Shrub originally from Central America reaching 5 metres in height. Leaves everlasting, opposite, ovate-elliptical up to 30 centimetres long, pale green in colour. Flowers pink tending to red and arranged in spiked

173

174

175

176

inflorescences up to 45 centimetres long which extend beyond the highest part of the branches. Flowers for most of the year.

PACHYCEREUS PRINGLEI (S.WATS.) BRITT. & ROSE [175]
(Cactaceae)

Very large cactus reaching 15 metres in height. Massive trunk up to a metre in diameter with 11-15 ribs.

Strong thorns in bunches of 20 or more measuring about 3 centimetres, with a slightly longer central spine. Flowers white, which can stay open by night as well as by day. Originally from New Mexico.

PLUMBAGO AURICULATA LAM. [176]
(Plumbaginaceae)

A climbing shrub with narrow, flexible stems. Leaves everlasting, from oblanceolate to slightly spatulate, up to

10 centimetres long. Flowers blue with paler hues, characterised by a long tube and expanded portion reaching 3.5 centimetres in diameter arranged in spherical inflorescences. Originally from Southern Africa but grown in many regions as a hedge species.

PODRANEA RICASOLIANA
(TANFANI) T. SPRAGUE [177]
(Bignoniaceae)

Creeping shrub originally from Southern Africa. Opposite, everlasting imparipinnate leaves up to 25 centimetres long and composed of 9-13 ovate leaflets, up to 10 centimetres long with pointed tip. Flowers pink streaked with red and arranged in subglobular inflorescences.

RAVENALA MADAGASCARIENSIS
SONN. [178]
(Strelitziaceae)

The "Travellers' Tree", as it is commonly known, is a gigantic herbaceous plant, reaching 16 metres in height. Originally from Madagascar. It seems that its name derives from the fact that travellers could always find fresh water inside its huge floral bracts and the flowers themselves. The trunk is simple or branched at the base and, like all the monocotyledons,

178

177

consists of the sheaths of the leaves wrapped round each other. The laminar leaf blade reaches 4 metres in length and is borne on equally long petioles which leave the trunk at approximately 45 degrees. The characteristic flowers are very similar to those of the other *Strelitziaceae.*

179

SENECIO CINERARIA DC. [179]
(Compositae)

An upright grass, stem woody at the base, up to 50-60 centimetres high, characterised by the tomentose, silver-grey hairs which cover it almost completely. Small, yellow composite inflorescences carried high on the stem.

SOLANDRA MAXIMA (SESSÙ & MOÙ.) P.S.GREEN [180]
(Solanaceae)

Woody climbing shrub originally from Mexico. Long-lasting, leathery, elliptical leaves briefly pointed at the tip and up to 25 centimetres long with long petiole. Very large yellowish flowers with brown veins in the inside, tube shaped and enlarging into a bell shape externally. Flowers throughout the year, except in full summer.

180

181

SPATHODEA CAMPANULATA BEAUV. 181 185
(*Bignoniaceae*)

Very beautiful tree due to its showy flowers which have given it the name of the "Tulip Tree". Medium sized tree no higher than 20 metres. Leaves long-lasting, pinnate, up to 65 centimetres long composed of up to 12 centimetre long leaflets. Bell shaped flowers, coloured bright red with golden yellow margins, up to 7 centimetres wide and grouped in globular inflorescenes at the tips of the branches. A rustic plant very suitable for growing along the roads.

STRELITZIA REGINAE BANKS EX DRYAND. 184
(*Strelitziaceae*)

Species of the genus *Strelitzia* originally from South Africa, are giant grasses which can reach 10 metres in height. The stem, as in the genus *Musa* (*Musaceae*) and *Ravenala* (*Strelitziaceae*) is herbaceous but wide in diameter and made up of the sheaths of the leaves which wrap around and fuse into one another. The leaf blades are very large, reaching 70 centimetres and are borne on a petiole which reach 2 metres in length. *S. reginae* or the "Bird of Paradise" is one of the smaller species since the floral scape does not exceed one metre and a half in height. The leaves can grow to 1.7 metres in length, including the petiole. Generally orange or yellow flowers with the lower portion a deep blue colour. One of the most employed species in horticulture as a pot plant and for cut flowers.

STRELITZIA NICOLAI REG. & KÙRN. 183
(*Strelitziaceae*)

Differs from *S. reginae* especially in size, where in this species it reaches its maximum for the genus. The floral scape can grow as high as 10 metres and the leaves 4 metres, of which 2 metres are part of the petiole. Flowers white with the bottom part varying from blue to purple. Flowers more or less continuously throughout the year.

TECOMA STANS (L.) HUMB. BOMPL. & KLOTZ. 182
(*Bignoniaceae*)

Shrub up to 6 metres high originally from Central and South America. The composite leaves are formed of 5-11 leaflets and reach 10 centimetres in length. Flowers yellow, bell shaped, clustered in inflorescences at the branch tips. Flowers the whole year through.

182

183

184

185

GLOSSARY

Abruptly pinnate = pinnate composed leaf ending in two leaves
Aerial root = root growing above the ground from the plant stem
Aerosol = suspended solid or liquid particles within a gas (e.g. mist or fog)
Alkaloid = nitrogenous basic substance found in plants; usually toxic but can be used at low doses in medicine
Alternate = (branches or leaves) arranged alternately on the two sides of the stem
Anther = part of stamen containing pollen
Anthropisation = transformation and alteration made by man to the land in order to render it suitable for his own interests and needs
Apical = pertaining to the apex, at the tip
Area = general area of distribution of a plant
Axil = angle between the upper side of a leaf and the stem on which it is borne

Basalt = dark green or grey brown igneous rock often in columnar strata
Berry = fruit with seeds enclosed in pulp
Biodiversity = multiplicity of the variety of living forms in a given area
Biogeography = science which studies the relationships between organism (and groups of organisms) and their geographical and ecological distribution
Blade = flattened, expanded part of leaf excluding petiole
Bract = small leaf or scale below calyx
Bulb = nearly spherical underground stem of lily, onion, sending roots downwards and leaves etc. upwards
Bush = shrub, clump of shrubs

Cactus = succulent plant with thick fleshy stem, usually no leaves and clusters of spines
Caducous = shed or falling off early
Calyx = outermost part of a flower consisting of sepals that may either be free as far as the base or partially joined
Canal = basal portion of calyx or corolla formed by sepals or petals fusing together
Carinate (or keel) = ridge on leaf
Caulis = plant axis carrying the leaves with function of support and conduction
Coenosis = biological community or group of living forms living and carrying out its function in a specified area
Community = see coenosis
Compound leaf = leaf composed of two or more similar parts
Coriaceous = leathery **Sub-coriaceous** = almost coriaceous
Cosmopolitan = with worldwide distribution

Culm = plant stem
Cultivar = cultivated as distinct from botanical variety of a plant
Cuticle = superficial film of plant
Cyathium = inflorescence typical of the family *Euphorbiaceae* consisting of a central female flower formed by a single pistil and peripheral male flowers formed by a single stamen and ensheathed by bracts

Deciduous = shedding leaves annually
Dichotomous = divided into two symmetrical bifurcation's
Dioic, dioecious = with male and female flowers on separate plants
Distal = away from centre of body or point of attachment, terminal (opposite = proximal)

Ecosystem = organisms and related physical surroundings in a specific area linked by a complex web of interchanges of energy and nutrients
Ellipse = regular oval
Elliptic = shaped like an ellipse
Elongate = slender or tapering in form
Endemic = species or genus regularly confined to a given region, continuously occurring in a particular area
Essential oils = aromatic oily substances
Evergreen = (tree, shrub) with green leaves the whole year through
Exotic = introduced from abroad

Flower-head = inflorescence consisting of several sessile flowers set in a receptacle at the end of a petiole, all at the same level and surrounded by one or more series of bracts
Formation = climax community of plants extending over a natural area determined by climate and growing forms of the individuals. e.g. pine-woods: a plant formation dominated by evergreen pine-trees

Genus = groups of animals or plant with common structural characteristics distinct from those of all other groups and usually containing several species
Glandular = (hair) when touched gives a viscous liquid
Glomerule = clustered flower-head
Graminaceous = like grass, grassy; with one or more culms with linear leaves

Habit (habitus) = natural mode of growth and consequent shape of plant
Habitat = natural home of plant or animal. It may be natural or artificial

Hair = elongated cell growing from epidermis: it can be short and conical-or long and cylindrical
Halophilous = ecological group comprising plants growing in soils rich in salt
Heliophilous = ecological group comprising plants which thrive under conditions of high light intensity
Herb = plant with stems that are not secondarily thickened and lignified (non-woody) and which die down annually
Honey-producing = plant preferably visited by bees (see melliferous)
Hyaline = glass-like, vitreous
Hybrid = offspring of two animals or plants of different species or varieties. It can be natural or artificial: in the latter case can be the base for cultivars

Inflorescence = arrangement and development of flowers on a flowering shoot
Infructescence = group of fruits deriving from flowers of the same inflorescence: sometimes resemble fruits (pineapple, blackberry etc.)
Involucre = whorl of bracts surrounding inflorescence

Lacinia = indentation or long narrow lobe in a leaf
Lacinated = cut into deep irregular segments, jagged, fringed
Lanceolate = shaped like a spearhead, tapering at the end
Latex = milky juice of a plant
Leaflets = parts of a composed leaf
Legume = fruit, edible part of leguminous plant
Liana = kind of climbing and twining tropical forest plant
Ligule = scale at the top of the leaf-sheath in grasses: similar to scape on a petal: strap-shaped corolla in composite plants
Ligulate = like a strap
Linear = (leaf) with long narrow shape
Living fossil = living organism belonging to systematic group specially represented by fossil forms of which has remained unchanged up to the present time since remote geological periods
Lobate = with lobes
Lobe = roundish and flat or pendulous part, often one of two or more such parts divided by fissure
Lobelia = herbaceous plant with blue, scarlet or purple flowers with deeply cleft corolla without spur

Melliferous = honey producing, plant preferably visited by bees
Microclimate = climate peculiar to a

specific situation which differs from the general climate of the region

Monocotyledon = division of flowering plants in which the embryo typically has one cotyledon or embryonic leaflet

Monospecific = consisting of only one species. Monospecies genus or monospecies habitat

Moorland = tract of open waste ground especially covered with heath

Mucronate = with pointed part or organ

Naturalised = said of plants originally not growing wild in a given region but which have become perfectly adapted to the area

Neo-tropical = phytogeographical region extending from Mexico to most of south America, as far as 40° latitude south

Nitrate = salt given by combination of nitric acid with base, or compound made by interaction of nitric acid and alcohol

Nitrophilous = plant growing well on soils rich in nitrate

Oblanceolate = (leaf) shaped like an upside-down lance; the widest part on the top, distal portion of the blade

Odd-pinnate = pinnate composed leaf consisting of an odd number of leaflets and ending with a single leaflet

Opposite = placed at the same height on opposite sides of stem, or placed straight in front of another organ

Orbicular = spherical, globular, rounded

Ovate = egg-shaped if solid or in outline, oval

Ovoid = solidly or superficially eggshaped, oval with one end more pointed

Paleoflora = plant species of past geological eras

Palm = slender tree with unbranched trunk and terminal crown of large evergreen leaves belonging to the order of Arecidae

Pancreatic juice = enzymes secreted by the pancreas

Palmate = shape of leaf with five lobes or segments spreading out from a common point

Panicle = branched flower head, each branch having several stalked flowers

Papilla = small fleshy projection on plant

Persistent = permanent

Petiole = leaf-stalk

Pinnate = with series of leaflets on each side of common petiole

Plates = continental masses in motion relative to each other, giving rise to oceans as they depart from one another and mountains and insular arches as they approach. Plate tectonics is the study of these movements and their results

Population = total number of inhabitants belonging to the same species living in a place in a certain time and able to interbreed

Prostrate = lying flat on the ground

Proteolytic enzyme = organic substance with protein origin favouring activation of many vital processes, in this case lysis of protein

Psamhalophyte = plant which can tolerate sandy and salty soils

Psammophyte = plant preferring sandy soils

Pseudotrunk = false trunks derived from leaf sheaths surrounding and fusing into each other

Pubescence = soft down on leaves and stem of plants

Pulses = edible seeds of leguminous plants, e.g. peas, beans, lentils

Quadrifoliate = four leaved

Raceme = flower cluster with separate flowers attached by short equal stalks at equal distances along central stem

Reniform = kidney-shaped

Revolute = with rolled back margin

Rhizome = underground stem often thick as in herbs and usually horizontal

Rootstock = underground part of a plant from which the roots and shoots grow

Rosette = circular cluster of leaves growing from base of a shoot

Runner = creeping stem that leaves main stem in plants like strawberry etc., and takes roots forming new growth at nodes or the tip

Savannah = treeless plain, great tracts of meadow like land

Saw-toothed = (leaves) with toothed margin like a saw

Scape = radical stem bearing fructification and no leaves as in primrose

Section = group, esp. subgenus

Sepals = one of the division of the calyx, calyx-leaf

Sessile = (of flowers, leaf etc.) attached directly by the base without stalk or petiole

Sheath = surrounding membrane or tissue

Shrub = woody plant smaller than a tree and usually divided into separate stems close to the ground

Spadix = spike of flowers closely arranged round fleshy axis and usually enclosed in a spathe

Spathe = large bract or pair of bracts enveloping spadix or flower cluster

Spatuliform = spatula-shaped, of an organ with large base and widening at the ends

Speciation = diversification of populations leading to formation of new species

Species = group subordinate in classification to genus and having members that differ only by minor details

Spike = flower cluster of many sessile flowers arranged closely on long common axis. Separate sprig of any plant on which flowers form spiked-like cluster

Stalk = stem, main axis of plant

Strigose = with short stiff hairs or scales

Succulent = thick and fleshy, having such leaves or stems

Tannin = astringent substance obtained mainly from bark of oak and other trees and used in preparing leather, ink and medicine

Tomentum = kind of pubescence composed of matted woolly hairs

Toothed = (leaf) margins with sharp teeth

Tree = perennial plant with single woody self-supporting stem or trunk usually for some distance above the ground

Trifoliate = leaves that are divided into three, as in clover

Trumpet-shaped = (flower or part of it: calyx or corolla) with funnel-shape, consisting of a tube with long and narrow basal part and wide distal part

Trunk = main body of tree, opposite of branches

Tuft = bunch, collection of grass, thorns etc. growing together at the base

Umbel = flower-cluster in which practically equally long stalks leave from a common centre to form a flat, convex or concave surface

Valve = segment into which capsule dehisces, each half of an anther after it opens

Variety = individual or group usually fertile with any other member of the species to which it belongs but differing in some characteristics, capable of perpetuation. Can be either a cultivated form (a cultivar) or naturally occurring

Verticil = whorl, set of parts radiating from axis

Vexillum = larger upper petal of papilionaceous flowers

Vicarious = species of other biological group sharing the same functions in differ places or habitats. the result of different groups of strictly related species which grow in different geographical areas; true vicarious species derive from a process of speciation due to geographic and reproductive isolation

Villous = covered with long soft hairs

Vulnerable = groups of species which the International Union for Conservation of Nature (I.U.C.N.) considers to be in danger of extinction if the causes of the fall in population does not end

Wedge-shaped = (leaf) with deep central rib, almost similar to a wedge

Xerophilous = adapted to hot and dry climate